CO-AZU-896

☐ NATIONAL GEOGRAPHIC
Reach
for Reading

COMMON CORE PROGRAM

NATIONAL GEOGRAPHIC

Hampton-Brown

Acknowledgments

Grateful acknowledgment is given to the authors, artists, photographers, museums, publishers, and agents for permission to reprint copyrighted material. Every effort has been made to secure the appropriate permission. If any omissions have been made or if corrections are required, please contact the Publisher.

Cover Illustration: Joel Sotelo

Cover Design and Art Direction: Visual Asylum

Illustration Credits: All PM illustrations by National Geographic Learning.

Photographic Credits: PM1.28 Photograph by Suzannah Weiss; PM1.29 Feije Riemersma/Alamy; PM2.28 Photograph by Brant Allen; PM2.29 AP Photo/Andy Eames; PM3.13 Anthony-MastersonFoodPix/Getty Images; PM3.14 William Higgins/Alamy; PM3.28 (l) PhotoDisc/Getty Images, ® BRUCE DAVIDSON/naturepl.com; PM5.13 Corbis; PM5.14 AFP.Stringer/ Getty Images; PM5.28 Sascha Burkard/Shutterstock; PM6.13 Album/ Paco Sanchez/Newscom; PM6.14 Rami Katzav; PM7.13 Getty Images; PM7.14 Tomas Kaspar/Alamy; PM7.28 Iwona Grodzka/iStockphoto; PM7.29 Bloomberg/Getty Images; 7.45 (tl) Jacek Chabraszewski/Shutterstock, (tc) paulaphoto/Shutterstock, (tr) Andy Dean Photography/Shutterstock; PM8.29 Bill Greene/The Boston Globe via Getty Images.

Visit National Geographic Learning online at www.NGSP.com

Visit our corporate website at www.cengage.com

Printed in the USA.

Globus Printing, Minster, OH

ISBN: 978-11338-99631

16 17 18 19 20 21

10 9 8 7 6 5 4

Contents

Unit 5: Mysteries of Matter

Unit 6: From Past to Present

Unit 7: Blast! Crash! Splash!

Unit 8: Getting There

Name _____ Date _____

How people help each other

Happy to Help

Make a concept map with the answers to the Big Question: How do people help each other?

For use with TE p. T3

PM1.1

Name _____ Date _____

Someone Who Needs Help

Make a story map about someone you know who needs help.

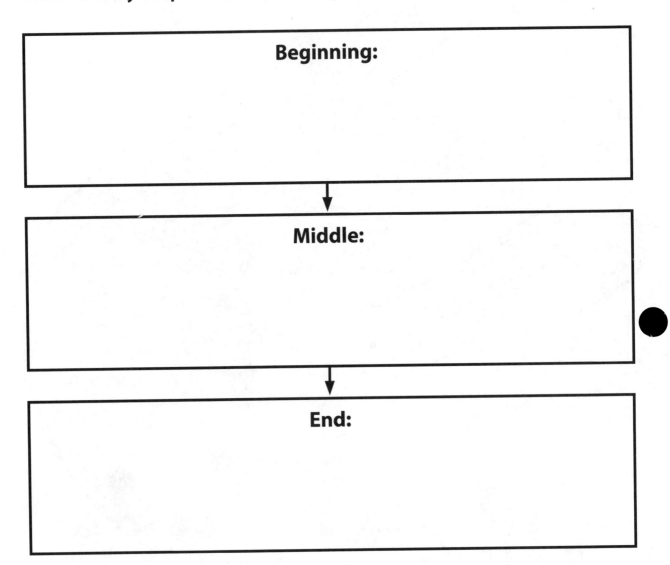

Beginning:

Middle:

End:

Grammar: Game

What's the Big Idea?

Directions:

1. Flip a coin. For heads, move 2 squares. For tails, move 1 square.

2. Tell if the noun you land on is **concrete** or **abstract**. Then use the noun in a sentence. If you name and use the word correctly, stay on your space. If not, move back one space.

3. Take turns. The player who reaches the end first wins.

START					END
sneaker		Is it a concrete noun?	Can you see it?		hot cocoa
fun	snow	Can you hear it?	Can you smell it?	kindness	fear
	backpack	Can you touch it?	Can you taste it?	cookie	
	health	Is it abstract?	Can you only think about it?	drums	
	love	stars	anger	friendship	

Edit and Proofread

Choose the Editing and Proofreading Marks you need to correct the passage. Look for the following:

- correct use of common and proper nouns
- correct use of capitalization

Editing and Proofreading Marks

∧	Add.
ℐ	Take out.
≡	Capitalize.
⊙	Add period.

    Today I walked into my new class. It was my first day at my new

school on ḻincoln Street. Mom said I would get over my fear. I didn't

feel any courage at first. I missed emily. She was my best Friend at

my old school.

    My new Teacher is mr. lang, and he asked rita to be my buddy

today. Rita smiled and said she would show me how to do things.

Pretty soon, I was feeling much better. Maybe Change isn't so bad

after all!

Test-Taking Strategy Practice

Know the Test Format

Directions: Read each question about "Those Shoes." Choose the best answer.

Sample

1 What does Jeremy buy with his own money?
Ⓐ snow boots
Ⓑ shoes for Antonio
● black-and-white shoes
Ⓓ blue shoes with cartoons

2 Why does Jeremy give his shoes to Antonio?
Ⓐ Jeremy does not like them.
Ⓑ Antonio needs new shoes.
Ⓒ Antonio asked Jeremy for his shoes.
Ⓓ Jeremy wants Antonio to be his friend.

Directions: Read the statement. Then write your answer in the space provided.

3 Explain why the new snow boots are better for Jeremy than the black-and-white shoes.

_____

_____

_____

 How did you use the test-taking strategy?

Name _____ Date _____

"Those Shoes"

Make a story map.

> **Beginning:**
> First, Jeremy wants new shoes, but they cost too much.

↓

> **Middle:**
> Next, Jeremy buys shoes that are too small.

↓

> Then, _____
> _____
> _____

↓

> **End:**
> Finally, _____
> _____
> _____

 Use your story map to summarize the story's plot for a partner.

Fluency Practice

"Those Shoes"

Use this passage to practice reading with the proper expression.

I have dreams about those shoes. Black high-tops.	8
Two white stripes.	11
"Grandma, I want them."	15
"There's no room for 'want' around here," Grandma says.	24
"What you *need* are new boots for winter."	32

From "Those Shoes," page 12

Fluency: Expression

1 ☐ Does not read with feeling.

2 ☐ Reads with some feeling, but does not match content.

3 ☐ Reads with appropriate feeling with most content.

4 ☐ Reads with appropriate feeling for all content.

Accuracy and Rate Formula
Use the formula to measure a reader's accuracy and rate while reading aloud.

_____ − _____ = _____
words attempted   number of errors   words correct per minute
in one minute   (wcpm)

Grammar: Reteach

Helping Hands

Grammar Rules: Nouns

A **common noun** names any **person**, **animal**, **place**, or **thing**.	My friend Berto wants to come along.
A **proper noun** names a particular **person**, **animal**, **place**, or **thing**. All important words in a proper noun start with a capital letter.	The soup kitchen is on Main Street.
A **concrete noun** names something you can see, hear, smell, touch, **or** taste.	table *(see)* cheers *(hear)*
An **abstract noun** names something you can **think about** but can't see, hear, smell, touch, or taste	goodness health joy

Write the noun with a capital or a small letter to complete each sentence correctly. Then find and underline the two abstract nouns.

1. Berto and I met the _____ at the soup kitchen.
   cook

2. Then _____ gave us things to do to help.
   mrs. chang

3. Many people came to the kitchen from _____.
   columbus street

4. Everyone said, "Thanks for your kindness, _____."
   dr. juarez

   Tell a partner about an activity you did with others. Include where you were and who was there. Explain which nouns you capitalized.

Game: Grammar

Tails for Reading

1. Copy the eight sets of sentences onto index cards. Have your partner do the same to make 16 cards.

2. Mix your cards with your partner's. Stack them face down.

3. Take turns turning over a card. Read the text and decide which **pronoun** best fits the blank. Read the sentence aloud. If your pronoun is correct, keep the card.

4. At the end of the game, the player with more cards wins.

Tucker is a cheerful dog. _____ likes kids.	Zoe is Tucker's sister. _____ is a tail-wagger.
The dogs visit schools. _____ listen as the children read.	Mrs. Mullaly likes dogs at her school. _____ says the program helps classes.
Kids who like the dogs say, "_____ love the visits!"	Mr. Chou volunteers in the program. "_____ set up visits," he says.
The school is careful. _____ has rules for safety.	Check out the program. _____ will like it!

Putting It Together

Rules for Playing "Putting It Together"

1. Take turns spinning the spinner.

2. Read the sentence part you land on. Add a subject or a predicate to make a complete sentence.

3. Write your sentence on paper.

4. Take five turns each.

5. Choose your three favorite sentences. Read them to another pair of students.

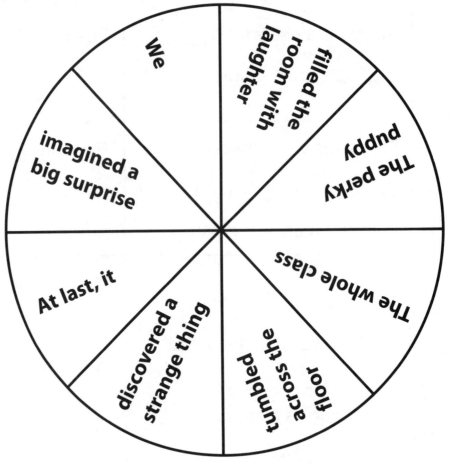

Make a Spinner

1. Put a paper clip over the center of the spinner.
2. Touch the point of a pencil on the middle of the wheel and through the loop of the paper clip.
3. Spin the paper clip to make a spinner.

Name _____ Date _____

Compare Genres

Compare a story and a poem.

	Story	Poem
It is arranged in lines.		✓
It has paragraphs.	✓	
It is usually long.		
It is usually short.		
It expresses the writer's feelings.		
The words sound like music.		

 Take turns with a partner. Ask each other questions about a story or poem.

Name _____ Date _____

Where's the Kitten?

Grammar Rules Complete Sentences

A complete sentence expresses a complete thought. It has a subject and a predicate.

Example: <u>A young girl</u> <u>has a small kitten.</u>

          ↑   ↑

       subject   predicate

Circle the complete sentence in each pair. Then copy correct sentences on the lines below to make a story.

1. My friend Maria.	My friend Maria has a kitten.
2. The kitten ran away.	Ran away.
3. Looked everywhere.	Maria looked everywhere.
4. Her sister Lisa helped her.	Her sister Lisa.
5. The girls found the kitten!	Found the kitten!

_____

_____

_____

_____

 Tell a partner about how you know each sentence is complete.

Name _____ Date _____

The Letter by Nikki Grimes

I sat frowning by my window

when the mail truck came today

with a letter from Danitra

who is many miles away.

I said mean things when she left me.

I was so mad at her then.

Was she writing to forgive me,

or to say I'm not her friend?

I ripped Danitra's letter open,

in spite of my worst fear.

I bit my lip until I read

"I wish that you were here."

Name _____   Date _____

The Lunchroom by Nikki Grimes

My lunch tray's like a boulder

I've lugged around for miles,

past strangers, left and right,

whose unfamiliar smiles

are meant for someone else

'cause I'm the new kid here.

"You'll do fine," Mom said earlier.

"Of that I have no fear."

At least, I have a pie

that I don't have to share.

If no one will sit next to me,

why should I even care?

Oh, wait! Here comes a boy.

"I'm Max," he says. "Who're you?"

I smile and introduce myself—

then break my pie in two.

Grammar: Grammar and Writing

Edit and Proofread

Choose the Editing and Proofreading Marks you need to correct the passage. Look for the following:

- incomplete sentences
- missing capital letters

Editing and Proofreading Marks

∧	Add.
℘	Take out.
≡	Capitalize.
⊙	Add period.

M
my friend Janet went out of town. One night, I. It was Janet's

neighbor. she said my friend's house was on fire! ran to her house.

The firefighters. They were battling the blaze. was worried about

Janet's dog. was still in the house! the firefighters did not know. I

told them. asked for the dog's name, so I told him. He smashed a

window. then he yelled, Buddy!" After a few minutes, Buddy! He

was safe.

was upset about her house. but she was happy, too. We had

saved her dog.

Grammar: Reteach

Ouch, That Hurt!

Grammar Rules: Pronouns and Complete Sentences

A **pronoun** takes the place of a <u>noun</u>.	<u>nurse</u> visits our school. **She** helps sick students.
Use a <u>subject</u> and a <u>predicate</u> to make a **complete sentence**. • A <u>subject</u> tells whom or what a sentence is about. It is usually a noun or a pronoun. • A <u>predicate</u> tells what the subject is, has, or does.	<u>Emily</u> <u>has</u> a cut. <u>She</u> <u>goes</u> to the nurse. The <u>nurse</u> <u>cleans</u> the cut. <u>Emily</u> <u>is</u> better.

Add words to make each of the following a complete sentence. Use capital letters correctly.

1. were playing soccer at school

_____

2. one of the players

_____

3. scraped his knees

_____

4. his best friends

_____

 With a partner, discuss why your sentences are complete.

Name _____ Date _____

Something That Has Improved

Make a comparison chart about something that has improved.

Before	Now

 Tell how you improved something. Tell how it was before and how it is now. Use the words *before*, *then*, *now*, and *after* to compare.

Grammar: Game

It's a Simple Story

Directions:

1. Copy the six sentences onto cards. Have your partner do the same. Mix your cards together and stack them face down.

2. **Round One:** Choose a card and read the sentence aloud. Draw one line under the simple subject. Draw two lines under the simple predicate.

3. **Round Two:** Shuffle all of the cards. Choose a card. Create a new sentence using either the simple subject or the simple predicate. Write it on the back of the card.

NOTE: In each round, if your partner agrees that you used the subject or predicate correctly, keep the card. Take turns until all the cards are used. The player with more cards wins the round.

My cousin Ben is a good reader.	The children in first grade hear Ben at the door.
The delighted teacher has a corner of the room for Ben.	Happy listeners sit on the rug around Ben.
He reads quietly to six children at a time.	The whole class has a new love of reading.

Grammar: Grammar and Writing

Edit and Proofread

Choose the Editing and Proofreading Marks you need to correct the passage. Look for the following:

- incomplete sentences
- missing capital letters

Editing and Proofreading Marks

∧	Add.
ℐ	Take out.
☰	Capitalize.
⊙	Add period.

Ben watched as his friends played soccer. ∧He wanted to play, too.

But Ben had asthma. is a disease. It makes it hard for people to

breathe. if he ran a lot. He knew it would be hard to play soccer.

wanted to try. His mom took him to Dr. Green. when he saw him.

Dr. Green said he could play! He gave Ben medicine to use. had to

take it before every practice.

after school the next day. It was his first practice. His friends. They

helped Ben with the rules. knew he could do it!

Name _____ Date _____

Know the Test Format

Directions: Read each question and choose the best answer.

Sample

1 In the sentence "It got me a <u>trip</u> to the principal's office," what does the word <u>trip</u> mean?

Ⓐ a fall

Ⓑ a map

Ⓒ a seat

● a journey

2 In the sentence "My motherand I <u>went over</u> the list until I knew those words," what do the words <u>went over</u> mean?

Ⓐ walked over

Ⓑ threw away

Ⓒ studied

Ⓓ forgot

Directions: Read the question. Then write a short answer below.

3 How does Henry find out he has dyslexia?

_____

_____

_____

 How did you use the test test-taking strategy to answer the question?

Comparison Chart

Compare Henry Before and Now

Show how Henry changed in "The World's Greatest Underachiever."

Before	Now
1. Henry had trouble spelling.	**1.** He writes books.
2. He didn't like school.	**2.**
3.	**3.**
4.	**4.**
5.	**5.**

 Use your comparison chart to retell the selection to a partner: Before, Henry _____. Now, he _____.

Fluency: Practice

"The World's Greatest Underachiever"

Use this passage to practice reading with proper intonation.

The next day, I went into the classroom and took out a sheet of paper.	15
Then Miss Adolf gave us the words. The first word was *carpet.*	27
I wrote that one down: *c-a-r-p-e-t.* I was feeling pretty confident.	38
Then came *neighbor*—I wrote down the letter *n.*	47
Then *rhythm*—I knew there was an *r. Suburban*—I wrote *s-u-b.*	59
My heart sank. I had gone from 100 percent to maybe a D-minus.	72
Where did the words go?	77

From "The World's Greatest Underachiever," pages 46–47

Intonation

1 ☐ Does not change pitch.

2 ☐ Changes pitch, but does not match content.

3 ☐ Changes pitch to match some of the content.

4 ☐ Changes pitch to match all of the content.

Accuracy and Rate Formula

Use the formula to measure a reader's accuracy and rate while reading aloud.

_____	−	_____	=	_____
words attempted in one minute		number of errors		words correct per minute (wcpm)

Name _____ Date _____

The Lion and the Mouse

Grammar Rules Sentences, Phrases, and Clauses

A **complete subject** is all of the words that tell about the subject.

A **simple subject** is the main word. It may be a **noun** or a **pronoun**.

A big, strong (lion) trapped a tiny gray mouse.

A **complete predicate** is all of the words in the predicate.

A **simple predicate** is the main word, which is the **verb**. (trapped)

A **phrase** is a group of words that does not have a subject and predicate.

within his big paws

A **dependent clause** has a subject and a verb but does not express a complete thought.

if you will let me go

Directions: Draw a line under a <u>complete subject</u> and two lines under a <u>complete predicate</u>. Circle a simple subject and simple predicate.

1. The golden lion released the mouse from his grasp.

2. The happy mouse promised the lion a favor in return.

Add words to make complete sentences. Capitalize correctly.

3. because the lion was tangled in a net

_____

4. with sharp little teeth

_____

Name _____ Date _____

Do They Agree?

Directions:

1. Flip a coin. For heads, move 2 squares. For tails, move 1 square.

2. Each time you land on a square, pick a NUMBER card. Tell if you have a singular or plural card. Create a sentence for the item you landed on. Then put the NUMBER card at the bottom of the stack.

3. If your sentence is correct, stay on your space. If not, move back one space. The player who reaches the end first wins.

Number Cards

1. Fold a tablet paper twice the long way. Keep it folded and fold the two ends together. Then unfold.

2. Print SINGULAR on 4 sections and PLURAL on 4. On the other side, write NUMBER on all 8 sections.

3. Cut apart the 8 sections.

4. Mix them up and stack them face down to play the game.

					leap	END
	is | are	player	dog		cousin	
	decide		growl		frog	
	zoom		team		find	
play	captain		scream	cat	has|have	
START	friend					

Grammar: Game

Working Together

Directions:

1. Read the sentence parts. Copy each one onto a separate index card.

2. After shuffling the cards, place them face down in two stacks: one for the subject cards and one for the predicate cards.

3. When it is your turn, choose a subject and a predicate. Read the cards as a complete sentence. Say the correct verb form.

4. If you are correct, keep the cards. Put them back if you are not. Then your partner takes a turn.

5. When the cards are all used, the player with more cards wins.

Subject	Predicate
Boys and girls	_____ everything for a gift basket. gather
Elly or Tran	_____ a gift with a tote bag. create
Dad or my brothers	_____ elderly people. visit
Mom or Dad	_____ to add a book. remember
Ty and Carol	_____ cocoa and a mug. include
The girls or Mom	_____ spices for the baskets. bring

Comparison Chart

Compare Points of View

Use a comparison chart to compare an autobiography and a biography.

"The World's Greatest Underachiever"	"Joseph Lekuton: Making a Difference"
• The narrator tells the story of _____ life.	• The narrator tells the story of _____ life.
• The narrator (is/is not) part of the story. (Circle one.)	• The narrator (is/is not) part of the story. (Circle one.)
• The selection is (an autobiography /a biography). (Circle one.)	• The selection is (an autobiography /a biography). (Circle one.)
• Examples of narrator's point of view:	• Examples of narrator's point of view:

 Take turns with a partner. Explain how you know that a selection is an autobiography or a biography.

Name _____ Date _____

We Like to Read

Grammar Rules Adding -s to Action Verbs	
• Use -s at the end of an action verb if the subject is *he, she,* or *it*.	Danny reads a story. He looks at the pictures.
• Do not use -s for *I, you, we,* or *they*.	I read to my friends. They look at the pictures.

Read each sentence. Write the correct form of the verb for each subject.

1. We _____ many stories.
   read / reads

2. I _____ autobiographies.
   like / likes

3. They _____ about real people.
   tell / tells

4. Henry Winkler _____ his own story.
   tell /tells

5. He _____ his problems in school.
   remember / remembers

6. His brain _____ differently.
   learn / learns

7. You _____ autobiographies, too.
   like / likes

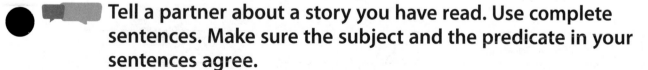 **Tell a partner about a story you have read. Use complete sentences. Make sure the subject and the predicate in your sentences agree.**

Name _____ Date _____

from

Facing the Lion by Joseph Lekuton

▲ Mission school

One of the problems the nomads have with school is that we move our villages and the cattle, but the school stays in one place. That means leaving the children behind. The first year, my village was near the school, and I was able to go home easily. In my second year, the missionaries built a dormitory and started a boarding school. My family could move wherever they wanted to, and I could stay in school.

My mom used to visit sometimes. She'd bring me milk. The food at school wasn't what I was used to, and there wasn't much of it. We ate mostly corn and beans—yellow corn, from America. Once I counted mine: There were 75 pieces of corn and 15 beans—so little it barely covered the plate. I didn't complain—I was grateful for the school and the missionaries—but I was a nomadic kid, raised on milk. So whenever my family was nearby, my mother would bring me some milk. Sometimes she'd walk 10 or 20 miles with it.

I went to that school through the seventh grade. Every time school closed for the vacation, I had to find my way home. That was one of the hardest things: The village might be 5 miles away, or it might be 50. Sometimes I wouldn't know exactly where my family was. I had to search for them.

Explanation: _____

_____

_____

_____

_____

Mark-Up Reading

Boy Between Two Cultures

by Olivia Hodgson

Because the Lekutons were nomads, their children faced special problems attending school. Nomads move around, but schools stay in the same place. During most of his school years, Joseph lived in a boarding school that missionaries had built. What a different life he had there! He bravely stayed behind at school when his family left.

▲ students in Rwanda, Africa

Joseph's mother visited him many times at boarding school. She wanted to see her son and also bring him milk. Joseph was used to drinking milk. After all, he had grown up in a cattle culture. But now he was in a new culture. The school offered him mostly beans and corn. The corn was strange to him. It was the yellow American kind. Also, the individual portions were small. Yet, Joseph saw it as his duty not to complain.

One of the bravest things Joseph had to do was to find his way home. When his school closed for vacation, Joseph didn't always know where his family was living. Sometimes, he traveled as much as 50 miles just to get home. By going home, he kept his ties to both cultures. He was still a student. Yet, when he was home, he was also learning to be a Maasai warrior.

Explanation: _____
_____
_____
_____
_____

Grammar: Grammar and Writing

Edit and Proofread

Choose the Editing and Proofreading Marks you need to correct the passage. Look for the following:

- subject-verb agreement
- correct use of forms of the verb **be**

Editing and Proofreading Marks

∧	Add.
⌐	Take out.
≡	Capitalize.
⊙	Add period.

We forms a clean-up team for our block. Meg lists our tasks. We vote on jobs and partners. Carly and Moira gets trash bags. Nate or the girls look for brooms. Juanita say she'll borrow gloves. We has a good team. I is proud to be a part of it.

Moms or dads brings snacks for us. My dog Rusty came with Dad, so Rusty are here. Is my big dog helpful? No, but he watchs! He have fun, too.

We is finished with our work! Meg or Rick rush to get a camera. We smile cheerfully!

Grammar: Reteach

Ants at Work!

Grammar Rules Subject-Verb Agreement

When a subject is **one** person or thing, the verb ends in **-s**.

An <u>ant</u> live<u>s</u> in a colony.

If the verb ends with **x**, **ch**, **sh**, **x**, or **z**, then the singular ends in **-es**.

<u>It</u> fix<u>es</u> up several rooms.

When a subject is **more than one**, the verb does <u>not</u> end in **-s**.

Many <u>ants</u> live together in one colony.

<u>Compound subjects</u> joined by **and** take a plural verb.

Workers **and** soldiers live in a colony.

<u>Singular compound subjects</u> joined by **or** take a singular verb.

A black ant **or** a red ant live<u>s</u> in a colony.

<u>Plural compound subjects</u> joined by **or** take a plural verb.

Sometimes black ants **or** red ants live in colonies of thousands!

Some verbs have special forms:	Each ant **has** a job to do.
has have am is are	Ants **are** very organized.

Read each sentence. Circle the correct verb.

1. An ant nest (has | have) rooms for different purposes.

2. A nursery and a resting place (is | are) two kinds of rooms.

3. Tunnels and rooms (keeps | keep) ants safe underground.

4. Worker ants (digs | dig) the tunnels in the ant nest.

Name _____ Date _____

Nature's Balance

Make a concept map with the answers to the Big Question:
What happens when nature loses its balance?

things that happen when nature loses its balance

Name _____ Date _____

Comparing Supplies

Compare the two pictures.

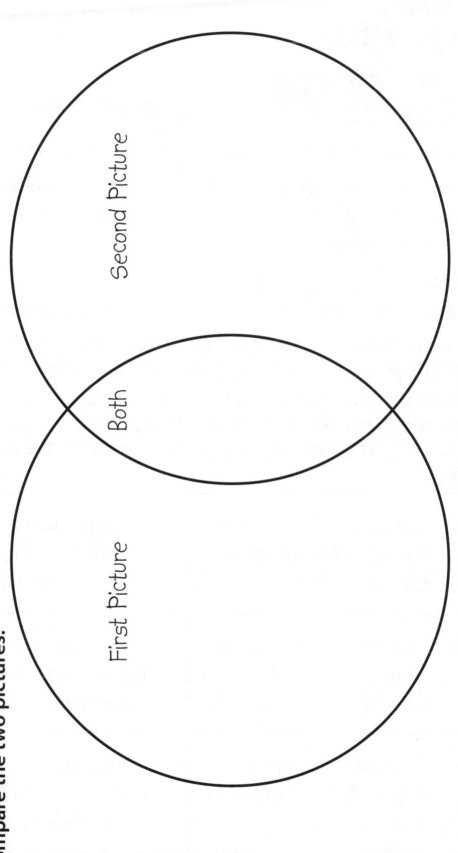

Second Picture

Both

First Picture

Take turns comparing and contrasting two different animals you know about.

Grammar: Game

"Says Who?"

Grammar Rules Dialogue

- Put quotation marks around the exact words of a speaker.
- Use a comma to set off a speaker's name. Also, use a comma after the speaker's name if the sentence continues.

Directions:

1. Write 1-6 on small pieces of paper. Mix the numbers face down.

2. Take turns turning over a number. Using different color pencils, each player fixes the dialogue punctuation for that number.

3. After each turn, check each other's use of quotation marks and commas. If you see a correction that needs to be made, see if your partner agrees. Then use your color to make the correction.

1.	How many bison live in the park? Lea asked the Yellowstone ranger.	**2.**	The number runs between 2,300 and 4,500 answered the ranger.
3.	Some bison die in harsh winters he added if they are young or old and sick.	**4.**	Are bison the largest land mammal in the country? asked Matt.
5.	They are! exclaimed the ranger. Bulls weigh up to 2,000 pounds!	**6.**	They can still run fast he said so don't ever try to get close to one.

Grammar: Grammar and Writing

Edit and Proofread

Choose the Editing and Proofreading Marks you need to correct the passage. Look for:

- capitalization of titles
- commas in addresses
- punctuation of dialogue

Editing and Proofreading Marks

∧	Add.
℘	Take out.
≡	Capitalize.
⊙	Add period.
∧,	Add comma.

"Ma, I have too many brothers and sisters! cried Reggie. "It's time

for me to move." Bunnies romped and giggled around him.

"Where will you go? Ma Rabbit asked.

"I read the book *New habitats for rabbits*," said Reggie, "and the

place I like best is Sandpoint Idaho."

"Come back often to visit us here in Elgin Illinois," said Ma.

I will," replied Reggie as he hugged Ma. "Right now, I have to

find my book *Hoppity's travels by Train and on foot*. It is the first thing

I'll pack.

Read Directions Carefully

Directions: Read the text. Then read the question and choose the best answer.

Sample

> Don Carlos wanted to serve snails in his restaurant. He gathered many, many snails. They crawled out of the restaurant and ate all the plants in the village. The villagers were very upset.

1 Why are the villagers upset?

Ⓐ Don Carlos is a bad cook.

Ⓑ The villagers don't want to eat snails.

● The snails caused trouble in the village.

2 Which of these events happen in "When the Pigs Took Over"?

Ⓐ Don Carlos says *"No Más"* when Alonzo and the villagers play music.

Ⓑ Alonzo refuses to help Don Carlos gather snails.

Ⓒ The pigs help the village.

Read the question. Then write a short answer below.

3 What does Don Carlos realize at the end of the story?

_____

_____

How did you use the test-taking strategy to answer the question?

"When the Pigs Took Over"

Compare Alonzo and Don Carlos.

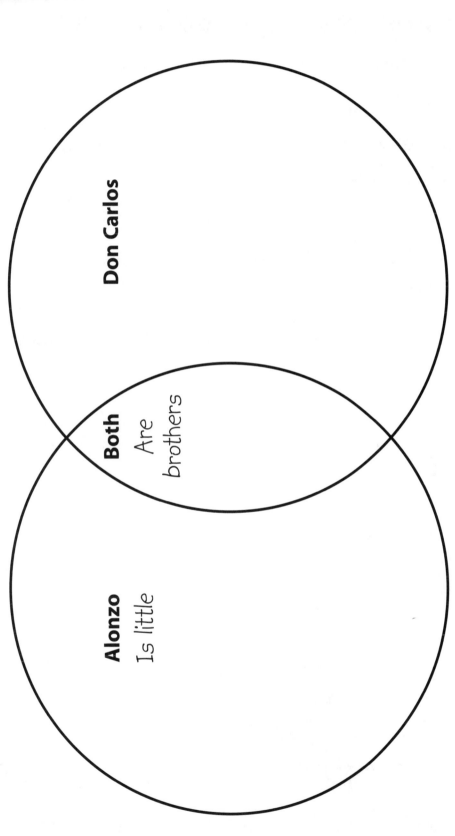

Don Carlos

Both
Are brothers

Alonzo
Is little

Talk with a partner about how the villagers are the same and how they are different.

Fluency Practice

"When the Pigs Took Over"

Use this passage to practice reading with the proper expression.

The pigs kept running wild.	5
Don Carlos put his hands over his ears. The music was more	17
than even he could stand. "¡No más!" he cried.	26
"¡Más!" Alonzo shouted to the villagers.	32
The villagers marched through the streets, playing louder	40
and louder.	42

From "When the Pigs Took Over," page 91

Expression

1 ☐ Does not read with feeling.

2 ☐ Reads with some feeling, but does not match content.

3 ☐ Reads with appropriate feeling with most content.

4 ☐ Reads with appropriate feeling for all content.

Accuracy and Rate Formula
Use the formula to measure a reader's accuracy and rate while reading aloud.

_____   −   _____   =   _____
words attempted   number of errors   words correct per minute
in one minute   (wcpm)

Grammar: Reteach

Helping Hands

Grammar Rules Titles, Addresses, and Dialogue

The first word and all important words in a title begin with a **capital letter**.	**B**orn **W**ild in the **S**mokies
Use a **comma** to separate parts of an address.	Gatlinburg**,** Tennessee
Quotation marks go around a speaker's exact words. One or two **commas** set off the speaker.	**"**We wanted to walk in woods**,"** she said**,** **"**and go fishing**."**

Read each sentence. Write in missing quotation marks and commas. Add the editing symbol (≡) to capitalize any small letters.

1. "Where did you go on vacation? asked Dion.

2. "We went to the Great Smoky Mountains" said Sari.

3. "My family used the gate in Cherokee North Carolina," she added.

4. "There are bears in the Smokies," said Dion. "Did you see any?

5. "We did see bears, cried Sari "but we didn't get close!"

6. "Did the park rangers show you a video called Day hiking and wildlife?" Dion asked. It gives good safety tips," he explained.

 Tell a partner about a place to visit. It can be very near or far from you. Think up a title for a book or video about the place and tell your partner which letters would be capitals.

Grammar: Game

Ask and Answer

Directions:

1. **Make the cards:** Copy each animal name onto separate cards. Mix the 16 cards and stack them face down. Make one question mark card and one period card. Place them face up next to the stack.

2. **Ask a question:** Player 1 chooses an animal card and the question mark and asks the player to the right a question about the animal. Examples: *What does a rabbit eat? What happens when there are too many fish?*

3. **Answer with a statement:** Player 2 takes the animal card from Player 1, picks up the period, holds the cards up, and answers with a statement. If players agree the statement is true, Player 2 keeps the animal card. If the statement is false, the card is returned to the stack.

4. **Ask the next question:** Player 2 chooses an animal card, holds the question mark, and asks Player 3 a question and so on. Continue for four rounds. Whoever has the most cards wins.

?	.		
bird	bee	rabbit	squirrel
snake	ant	fish	frog

Game: Grammar

That's a Problem! Fix It.

Directions:

1. Each square has the name of a plant or animal. It also has the name of something that can be a problem if it is out of balance.

2. Two teams each have a player toss a marker at the same time.

3. As quickly as they can, partners on a team write an exclamation and a command about the two items in their square. The exclamation tells how the two things are out of balance. The command tells how to fix the problem.

   Examples:
   The cows are fat from too much corn!
   Feed them less corn.

4. The first team to write an exclamation and command gets a point. Play five rounds. The team with more points wins.

squirrels	grass	rabbits
nuts	water	carrots
cows	sheep	birds
corn	grass	seeds
bees	house plants	flowers
flowers	sun	weeds

Name _____ Date _____

Compare Genres

Use this chart to compare a humorous story and a riddle.

	Humorous Story	Riddle
funny	✓	✓
usually long		
short		
playful language		
paragraphs		
questions and answers		

 Talk with a partner about which kind of humorous selection you liked better—the story or the riddles. Tell your partner why you liked one more than the other.

Grammar: Reteach

Helping Hands

Grammar Rules Kinds of Sentences

A **statement** tells something.	I have a pet bird.
An **exclamation** shows strong feeling.	He is so funny!
A **command** tells someone to do something.	Look at this picture of him.
A **question** asks something.	Do you have a pet?
Sometimes the answer to a question has a **contraction**.	No, I **don't**. No, it **isn't**.

Read each sentence. Write C for command, S for statement, E for exclamation, and Q for question. Then underline the contractions.

1. Do you like corn?   _____

2. No, I don't.   _____

3. I really love corn!   _____

4. Some birds like it, too.   _____

5. Where do they find corn?   _____

6. It's in the bird feeder.   _____

7. Wow! Look at all that corn!   _____

 Write a statement, a question, and an exclamation about something that happened today. Read your sentences to your partner.

Be Careful What You Wish For
by Katie Owens

Farmer Ray's crops had not felt a drop of rain in months. One day, Ray noticed a purple cow stuck in a thorny bush. "Help!" cried the cow. "I can't mooooove." Farmer Ray freed the cow. In return, the cow granted him three wishes.

"Let it rain buckets tomorrow!" Ray ordered.

The next morning, Ray sprang from bed and ran to the window. His fields were covered with shiny metal buckets. "No!" he shouted.

> **Explanation:** _____
> _____

Furious, Ray rushed outside to find the cow. "Looks like someone's in a bad mooood," said the cow.

"Of course I am!" Ray cried. "I meant that I wanted a lot of rain!"

"Really?" said the cow. "Well, at least you have two wishes left."

"What I want is nice weather so my crops can grow! OK?"

"Very well," said the cow.

The next morning, Ray sprinted out the door and stopped in his tracks! There was still no rain, and the heat was unbearable.

A voice bellowed from above. "Good morning, Farmer Ray. You look very handsome today!" Ray saw the sun smiling down at him. The weather was being nice to him, but his crops were burning up!

> **Explanation:** _____
> _____

Mark-Up Reading

(continued)

Ray was furious. "I don't want the weather to be nice to me! I just want nice weather!" He threw down his hat and stomped on it.

"So that's the thanks I get," the cow grumbled.

"Forget weather, cow! Just give me a thousand **bucks**!"

Ray went to sleep that night dreaming of money. When he awoke the next morning, Ray could not believe his eyes. A huge herd of male deer was grazing on what was left of his crops.

"Silly cow!" Ray shouted. "I need money, not deer!"

Explanation: _____
_____

The cow apologized for this new mix-up. "I tell you what," he said, "since things have gone so badly, I'll throw in a bonus wish. Now be careful what you wish for!"

"No thanks," Ray said. "Something always goes wrong." He walked off muttering to himself, "I just wanted everything to come up roses."

"Interesting wish," the cow said, and then vanished.

The next morning, Farmer Ray got up and looked out the window. In every direction, his fields were covered with red roses.

This time, Ray smiled. "It looks like I'm in the flower business now."

Explanation: _____
_____

In Other Words

bucks dollars

Grammar: Grammar and Writing

Edit and Proofread

Choose the Editing and Proofreading Marks you need to correct the passage. Look for the following:

- sentences that begin with capital letters
- sentences that end with correct punctuation marks

Editing and Proofreading Marks

↑!	Add exclamation.
ℐ	Take out.
≡	Capitalize.
⊙	Add period.
∧	Add comma.

Experts thought there were no more ivory-billed woodpeckers?

they thought they were extinct. The last time one was spotted was

in 1944? Then a logging company cut down the trees around its

home. Wildlife experts thought that was the end for the bird

Sixty years later, they got a great surprise A person was kayaking

in an Arkansas forest He said he saw an ivory-bill? tell us if you

agree that was a big surprise Many scientists traveled there. Were

they able to find an ivory-billed woodpecker. Sadly, no. But scientists

believe they might be there. The ivory-billed woodpecker could be

back from extinction

Grammar: Reteach

Tiger Conservation

Grammar Rules Kinds of Sentences

There are four kinds of sentences with four purposes. All begin with capital letters.

- A **statement** tells something. It ends with a **period**.
  Scientists fear tigers will die off.

- A **question** asks something. It ends with a **question mark**.
  Could tigers vanish forever?

- An **exclamation** shows strong feeling. It ends with an **exclamation mark**.
  What a terrible loss that would be!

- A **command** tells someone what to do. It can end with a **period** or an **exclamation mark**.

Read each sentence. Use proofreading symbols to fix all errors in capitalization and punctuation. Then write the kind of sentence it is on the line.

1. three types of tigers are already extinct _____

2. save forests and jungles for the tigers _____

3. Are tiger's stripe patterns unique _____

4. yes, they're like fingerprints _____

5. make a poster to help save tigers _____

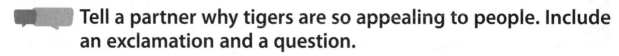 Tell a partner why tigers are so appealing to people. Include an exclamation and a question.

Ecosystem Alert

Make a cause-and-effect diagram of an ecosystem that is out of balance.

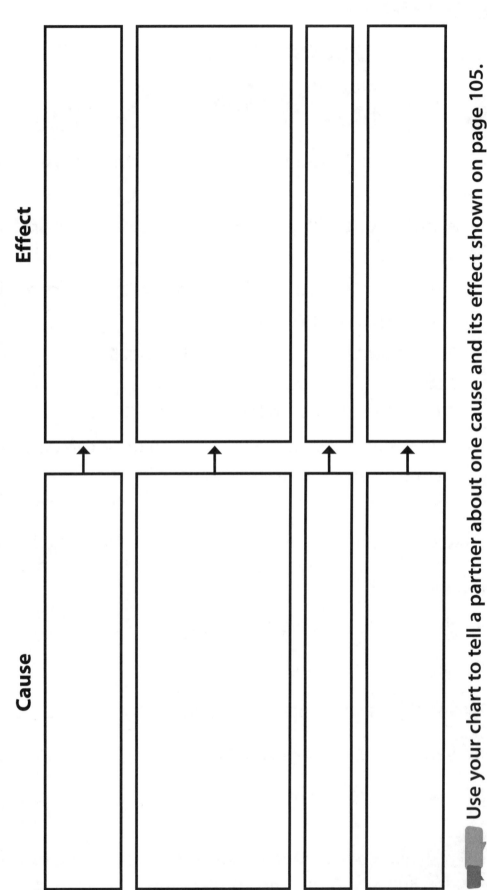

Cause

Effect

Use your chart to tell a partner about one cause and its effect shown on page 105.

PM2.17

Name _____ Date _____

It's Quite Simple!

Directions:

1. Spin for a subject. Then choose a predicate.

2. Write a **simple sentence** using the subject and predicate.

3. Take turns until you each have 4 sentences.

4. Review each other's sentences. Give one point for each sentence that starts with a capital letter and ends with the correct punctuation. Give another point if the statement is true.

Make a Spinner

1. Put a paper clip at the center of the circle.

2. Put the point of a pencil through the opening of the paper clip and at the center of the circle.

3. A player holds the pencil in place and spins the paper clip to choose a subject.

Subjects

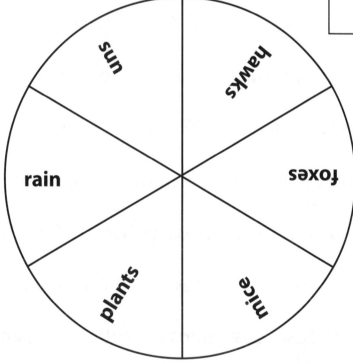

Predicates

shines on plants	nibble on seeds and plants
provides water for life	hunt through fields for mice
grow in soil	dive from the sky to catch mice

Edit and Proofread

Choose the Editing and Proofreading Marks you need to correct the passage. Look for the following:

- contractions correctly spelled
- correct use of simple sentences and simple sentences with compound subjects and compound predicates

Editing and Proofreading Marks

∧	Add.
✐	Take out.
≡	Capitalize.
⊙	Add period.
∨	Add apostrophe.

An emu grows up to 6 feet tall. ~~An emu~~ **and** weighs up to 120 pounds.

Although its a bird, an emu doesnt fly. An emu does have strong

legs! An emu uses them to run 30 miles an hour!

The emu is part of Australia's ecosystem. It eats insects, seeds, and

plants. Then it spreads seeds across it's habitat. Emus' habitat once

covered most of Australia, but they cann't live in urban areas. Emus

are'nt seen on the East Coast. Emus are extinct in Tasmania.

Now farmers help. Rural areas did'nt have enough water, but

ranchers now provide water. Livestock can drink the water. Emus can

drink the water. Emus have a new habitat!

Name _____ Date _____

Read Directions Carefully

Directions: Read each question about "When the Wolves Returned." Choose the best answer.

Sample

1 Read each sentence below. Then choose the one that states a fact about the food chain in Yellowstone correctly.

● Wolves were at the top of the food chain.

Ⓑ Pronghorn fawns ate trees that elk needed for food.

Ⓒ Coyotes and beavers competed for the same food.

Ⓓ With no food, ducks almost disappeared from the park.

2 Which sentence tells what happens first?

Ⓐ Beavers almost disappeared from the park.

Ⓑ Coyotes disappeared from the park.

Ⓒ Hunters killed the wolves.

Ⓓ Elk ate trees and shrubs.

Directions: Choose the answer that best completes each sentence.

3 Beavers began to disappear from the park because _____.

Ⓐ the coyotes ate only small animals

Ⓑ the wolves ate the elk and deer

Ⓒ the elk ate young trees

Ⓓ hunters killed them

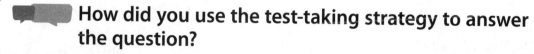 **How did you use the test-taking strategy to answer the question?**

Name _____ Date _____

"When the Wolves Returned"

Complete this chart as you reread "When the Wolves Returned."

Cause	Effect

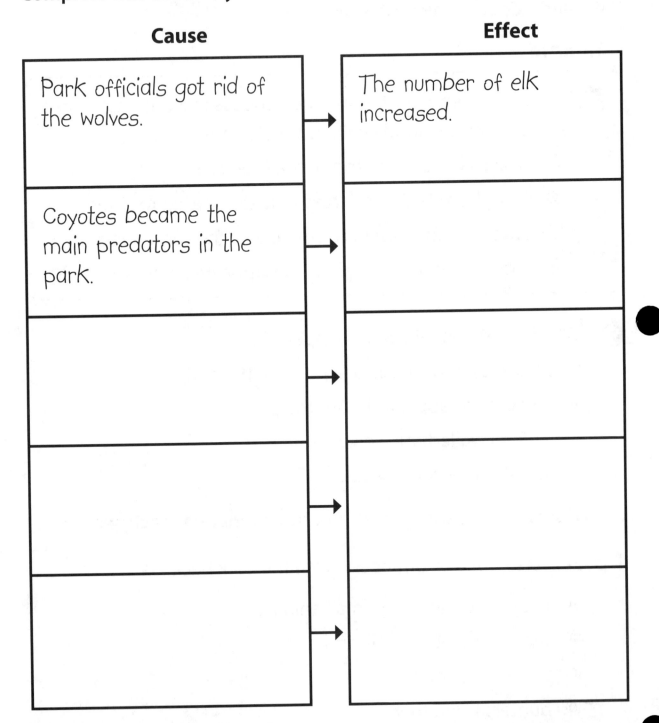

Cause	Effect
Park officials got rid of the wolves.	The number of elk increased.
Coyotes became the main predators in the park.	

 Tell a partner about causes and effects in the selection that surprised you.

Name _____   Date _____

"When the Wolves Returned"

Use this passage to practice reading with proper phrasing.

The purpose for making Yellowstone a national park was to	10
protect its natural wonders for visitors. People enjoyed seeing	19
animals in the park, too, like elk and deer. But wolves fed on	32
them. So, hunters were paid to kill the wolves. Park officials did	44
not understand that killing the wolves would throw nature out	54
of balance.	56

From "When the Wolves Returned," page 113

Phrasing

1 ☐ Rarely pauses while reading the text.   3 ☐ Frequently pauses at appropriate points in the text.

2 ☐ Occasionally pauses while reading the text.   4 ☐ Consistently pauses at all appropriate points in the text.

Accuracy and Rate Formula
Use the formula to measure a reader's accuracy and rate while reading aloud.

_____ − _____ = _____
words attempted   number of errors   words correct per minute
in one minute   (wcpm)

Grammar: Reteach

Grasshoppers and Beetles

Grammar Rules Contractions and Simple Sentences

- A **contraction** is a shortened form of two words. It uses an **apostrophe** to show where one or more letters is left out.

    it's   you'll   can't   isn't

- A **simple sentence** has one independent clause.
  The <u>boys</u> <u>plan</u> a science report.

- A **compound subject** has <u>two or more simple subjects</u> that have the same predicate.
  <u>Li</u> **and** <u>Lon</u> <u>look</u> for subjects.

- A **compound predicate** has <u>two or more simple predicates</u> that have the same subject.
  Li <u>plans</u> his re port **and** <u>looks</u> for a video.

- Compounds are joined by *and* or *or* .

Write each item as a simple sentence with a compound subject or a compound predicate. Correct errors in contractions.

1. I can do a video on grasshoppers. I can write a report on beetles.

_____

2. Grasshoppers are insects. Tiger beetles are insects.

_____

3. Grasshoppers live everywhere. They like many habitats.

_____

Grammar: Game

Combine the Clauses

Directions:

1. Toss a marker onto an independent clause. Choose a dependent clause that makes sense with it. Combine them and read them aloud.

2. Tell which word is capitalized and how the sentence is punctuated.

3. A player gets one point for each correct use of a dependent clause and one point for correct capitals and punctuation.

4. Take turns until all dependent clauses have been combined with independent clauses. The winner is the player with the most points.

Independent Clauses

striped bass can live in the salty ocean and in fresh water	striped bass numbers had once dropped too low
they are easy to recognize	a fisher has to throw it back into the water
I feel I have been a good sportsman	I can't pull in a fully grown, 50-pound bass

Dependent Clauses

because of pollution, loss of habitat, and overfishing	although many fish live only in saltwater *or* in fresh water
until a little striped bass reaches a bigger size	since striped bass have 12 to 16 stripes
if I let a small fish go	unless I have help

Grammar: Game

Coordinate Your Ideas

Directions:

1. After choosing an idea from the circle, Player 1 uses it to state an independent clause.

2. Player 2 spins the paper clip to choose a conjunction, then uses it to add an independent clause to Player 1's sentence.

3. If players agree that a compound sentence has been formed correctly, play continues. If not, players correct the sentence. Remember: use *and* when joining similar ideas, *but* when joining different ideas, and *or* when joining choices.

4. After a few rounds, write two of your favorite compound sentences. Trade papers with other players to look for correct use of capitals, commas, and end punctuation.

Make a Spinner

1. Put a paper clip over the small circle at the center of the triangle.

2. Put a pencil point through the opening in the paper clip.

3. Spin the paper clip to choose a conjunction.

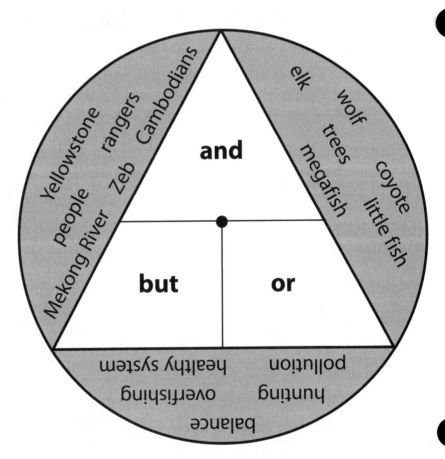

Name _____ Date _____

Compare Ecosystems

Compare Yellowstone Park and the Mekong River.

Yellowstone Park	Mekong River
Is in the United States	Is in Cambodia

 Tell your partner which ecosystem you would rather visit and why.

Grammar: Practice

Pets for Aziz

Grammar Rules Compound Sentences

You can use *and*, *but*, or *or* to combine two short sentences into one long compound sentence.

1. Use *and* to join ideas that are alike.

    *Dogs are friendly, **and** they make good pets.*

2. Use *or* to join ideas that are different.

    *Dogs like to be with people, **but** cats often like to be alone.*

3. Use *or* to join ideas that show a choice.

    *You might like to have a dog, **or** you might rather have a cat.*

Use *and*, *but*, or *or* to complete each compound sentence.

Aziz loves animals, ___*and*___ he has several pets. His dog

sleeps in the kitchen, _____ his two cats sleep there, too.

Some dogs and cats fight each other, _____ his play together

every day. Aziz wants to get a snake, _____ maybe he would

choose a lizard instead. He asked his mother to buy a snake for

him, _____ she said no. She doesn't like snakes, _____ she

doesn't want another pet. Maybe Aziz should ask again, _____

maybe he should just visit the zoo!

 Tell a partner about different kinds of pets. Use compound sentences.

Mark-Up Reading

Would You Rather Be a FISH?

from *National Geographic Kids*

National Geographic Kids asked scientist Zeb Hogan about his work, his heroes— and what kind of fish he would like to be!

NG Kids: What's a normal day like for you?

Hogan: When I am **in the field**, I spend almost all of my time on or near the water.

▲ Zeb Hogan holds a giant Eurasian trout.

In Southeast Asia, I rely on fishers to help gather the information that I need. We own a small boat and take it along the river to meet with as many fishers as possible. If the fishers catch an endangered fish, we work with them to get the fish tagged and released back into the water. I also interview all the fishers that I meet to ask them about their catches and the abundance of endangered species.

In Mongolia, we work with recreational fishers to gather information about the ecology of the world's largest trout. In a typical day, we wake up at 7 A.M., go out on the river about 9 A.M., spend the day tagging and releasing fish, return to camp at 6 P.M., clean up, and eat.

How Details Support Main Idea _____

_____

In Other Words

in the field out collecting data for research

Mark-Up Reading

Would You Rather Be a FISH? (continued)

NG Kids: Do you have a hero?

Hogan: Nowadays, my heroes are people who are passionate about working to make the world a better place. Personally, I have a special feeling for anyone who loves rivers and aquatic life. I am even more impressed by everyday people that I meet who show a love for animals and the environment. Kids are great in the sense that they have a love and curiosity about animals and the outdoors.

> **How Details Support Main Idea** _____
>
> _____
>
> _____

NG Kids: If you were a fish, what kind would you want to be?

Hogan: Fish in most parts of the world have a tough life. Fish like the Mekong giant catfish, the Chinese paddlefish, and the Murray cod are in danger of extinction and have to deal with all kinds of challenges. They have to deal with water pollution, avoid being caught and eaten, navigate around dams and irrigation canals (often impossible), and find a mate. It's nearly impossible for them to survive. So…if I had to be a fish I'd like to be a giant Eurasian trout living in a remote area.

▲ Hogan measures a giant carp in Cambodia.

> **How Details Support Main Idea** _____
>
> _____
>
> _____

Name _____ Date _____

Edit and Proofread

Choose the Editing and Proofreading Marks you need to correct the passage. Look for correct usage of the following:

- complete sentences
- correct compound sentences
- correct use of capitals and punctuation

Editing and Proofreading Marks

∧	Add.
✗	Take out.
≡	Capitalize.
⊙	Add period.
∧	Add comma.

               ,and

Pollution is harmful∧overuse of an ecosystem is harmful, too.

Ecosystems are hurt by bad decisions as well. Because ecosystems can be harmed in different ways. We need different solutions for them.

A harmful decision was made to kill all wolves in Yellowstone. The park system became unbalanced. Because the wolves were gone. Since they have returned. The park system is in balance. The park is healthier or people enjoy visiting.

Overuse is a problem, too. Mekong River has fewer megafish, or one reason is overfishing. You can't tell people not to fish. And you can limit the size they keep.

Balance is difficult to keep in any ecosystem or we have to keep trying!

Connected to the Great Lakes

Grammar Rules Clauses and Compound Sentences

• An **independent clause** can stand alone as a sentence. • A **dependent clause** cannot stand alone. A **signal word** connects it to an independent clause. • If the dependent clause comes first, it is followed by a **comma**.	**Signal Words** *before*　　　*after* *although*　　*unless* *since*　　　*because* *until*　　　*if* *even if*　　*as if* *so that*　　*when*
• Use the conjunction *and, but,* or *or* to join two independent clauses to make a **compound sentence**. Use a **comma** before the conjunction.	Join equal <u>similar</u> ideas with *and*. Join equal <u>different</u> ideas with *but*. Join equal ideas that are <u>choices</u> with *or*.

Combine the clauses. Use correct capitalization and punctuation.

1. There are five Great Lakes. and the largest is Lake Superior.

_____

2. If we enter Lake Ontario on the east. we can go through all five.

_____

3. Four lakes are partly in Canada. But Lake Michigan is not.

_____

Name _____ Date _____

amazing things about plants

Unit Concept Map

Life in the Soil

Make a concept map with the answers to the Big Question: What is so amazing about plants?

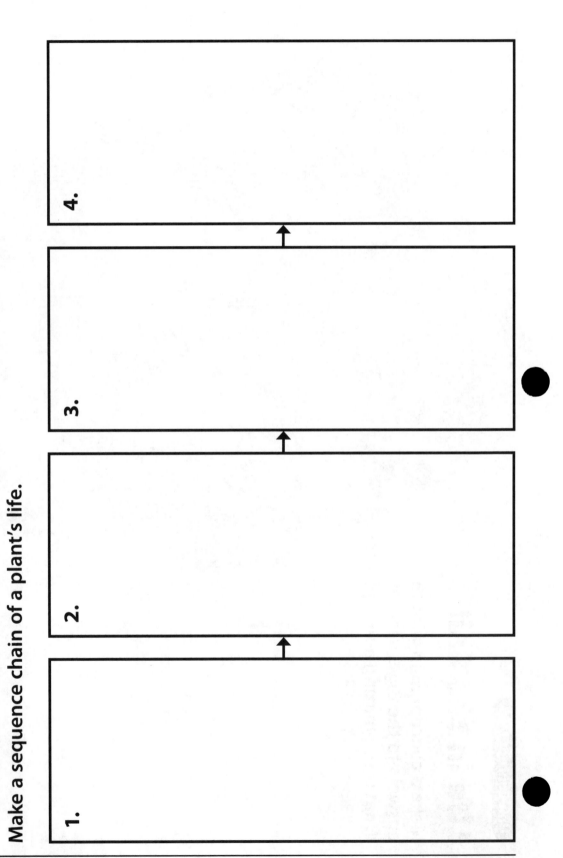

Grammar: Game

Life Is Complex

Plural Nouns Complex Sentences

1. A complex sentence has an <u>independent clause</u> and one or more <u>dependent clauses</u>.

   <u>The rain poured down</u> <u>until all of the plants were soaked.</u>

2. If the dependent clause comes first, put a comma after it.

   <u>When it quit raining,</u> <u>we ran outside</u> <u>so we could see our plants.</u>

1. **Play with a partner.**
2. **Spin the spinner.**
3. **Add a dependent clause to an independent clause.**
4. **Or add an independent clause to a dependent clause.**
5. **The first player to create five correct sentences wins the game.**

Make a Spinner

1. Put a paper clip over the center of the spinner.
2. Put the point of a pencil through the loop of the paper clip.
3. Your partner holds the pencil while you spin for your turn.

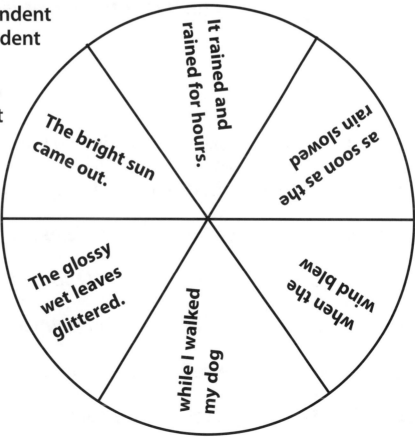

Grammar: Grammar and Writing

Edit and Proofread

Choose the Editing and Proofreading Marks you need to correct the passage. Look for the following:

- correct use of conjunctions and dependent clauses
- correct use of independent clauses
- correct use of punctuation

Editing and Proofreading Marks

∧	Add.
ℐ	Take out.
∧,	Add comma.
∧.	Add period.
/	Make lowercase.

"Last year, we didn't eat many of our own garden vegetables,ℐ because the pests ate most of them," said Maggie sadly. "Although we tried to keep them out. They were very clever."

Andy replied, "I liked seeing rabbits and deer. When they came to eat."

"I did too," Maggie said, "but gardening is a lot of work. Unless we can get more for our efforts I may not want to plant this year."

"Before we plant seeds we can build a fence," suggested Andy.

"Good idea, Andy," said Maggie. "We could also plant veggies outside the fence. Animals can eat those, whenever they want too!"

"We won't have to weed. The area outside the fence!" Andy was excited. "As soon as we can buy the supplies. We'll get started."

Look for Important Words

Directions: Read each question about "Two Old Potatoes and Me." Choose the best answer.

Sample

1 What happens before the girl and her dad plant the potatoes?

   Ⓐ The potato plant turns brown.

   ● The girl finds two old potatoes.

   Ⓒ The girl digs up some potatoes.

   Ⓓ The potato plant grows violet blossoms.

2 Why will the island be a good place for families to live?

   Ⓐ sunshine

   Ⓑ shade

   Ⓒ rocks

   Ⓓ insects

3 Why does the girl carry a big bucket to the garden?

   Ⓐ There are so many potatoes.

   Ⓑ So she can give it to Grandpa.

   Ⓒ She has lots of tools to carry.

   Ⓓ They want to plant more potatoes.

 Tell a partner how you used the strategy to answer the questions.

Sequence Chain

"Two Old Potatoes and Me"

Make a sequence chain of "Two Old Potatoes and Me."

1. A girl finds two potatoes with sprouts.

2. She and her dad plant them.

3.

4.

5.

6.

7.

Use your sequence chain to retell the story to a partner.

© National Geographic Learning, a part of Cengage Learning, Inc.
For use with TE p. T164a

PM3.6

Fluency: Practice Expression

"Two Old Potatoes and Me"

Use this passage to practice reading with proper expression.

"Gross." I tossed them in the trash.	7
"Wait," Dad said. "I think we can grow new potatoes with those.	19
I'll call your grandpa. He'll know."	25
Dad and I talked with Grandpa. Then we took the potatoes to the	38
sunniest spot in the garden.	43

From "Two Old Potatoes and Me," pages 152-153

Expression

[1] ☐ Does not read with feeling.　　　　[3] ☐ Reads with appropriate feeling for some content.

[2] ☐ Reads with feeling, but does not match content.　　[4] ☐ Reads with appropriate feeling for all content.

Accuracy and Rate Formula
Use the formula to measure a reader's accuracy and rate while reading aloud.

$$\underset{\substack{\text{words attempted} \\ \text{in one minute}}}{\underline{\hspace{3cm}}} - \underset{\text{number of errors}}{\underline{\hspace{3cm}}} = \underset{\substack{\text{words correct per minute} \\ \text{(wcpm)}}}{\underline{\hspace{3cm}}}$$

Grammar: Reteach

Unusual Blooms

Grammar Rules Collective Nouns

- A complex sentence has an <u>independent clause</u> and one or more <u>dependent clauses</u>.
- The dependent clause begins with a conjunction.
- If the dependent clause comes first, put a comma after it.
- The conjunction makes a clear connection between ideas in the clauses.

  <u>When my pen pal sent me a pack of seeds</u>, <u>he told me to share them with friends.</u>

  <u>I gave seeds to everyone until I had just a few for myself.</u>

- **Underline the independent clauses.**
- **Circle the dependent clauses.**
- **Box the conjunctions, and add a comma if it is needed.**
- **Write a final, complex sentence.**

1. I planted my seeds in rich soil while the sun was still bright.

2. When daylight came each day I watered the little round seeds.

3. Then shoots sprang up and grew until they were strong vines.

4. I went to my garden one night so I could see it by moonlight.

5. I was surprised because I saw flowers blooming in the night!

6. _____

 Tell a partner about an unusual plant you have seen, or make up a description of one. Use at least one complex sentence.

Grammar: Game

How Many?

Directions:

1. Play with a partner.

2. Use an eraser, paper clip, or other small object as a game piece.

3. Flip a coin to move:
   Heads = 1 space forward   Tails = 2 spaces forward

4. Read the noun aloud. Say the plural form and then spell it. If your partner agrees that you are correct, stay on your new space. If you don't, go back one space.

5. Take turns. The first player to reach the END wins!

basket	waltz	wish	stream	miss	END
fox					
coach					
glass	field	sash	building	class	garden
					potato
					bench
BEGIN	farmer	bush	mountain	fox	plant

Grammar: Game

Toss and Spell

Directions:

1. Play with a partner. Take turns tossing a game marker into one of the word squares.

2. Write the plural form of the noun on another paper. Check the spelling. If it is correct, write your initials in the square.

3. Each partner takes six turns. Then you each count all of the squares with your initials. Who has more?

berry	**Friday**	**story**
chimney	**penny**	**family**
cherry	**valley**	**monkey**
activity	**turkey**	**dictionary**

Compare Genres

Compare a story and a haiku.

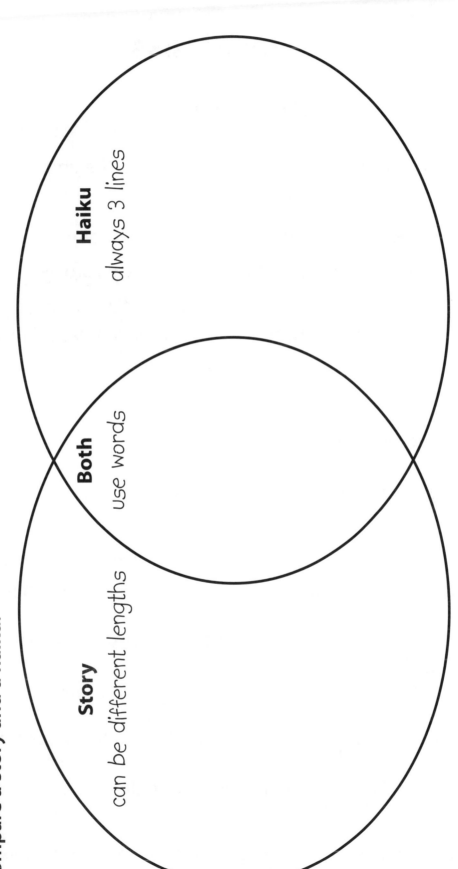

Haiku
always 3 lines

Both
use words

Story
can be different lengths

Take turns with a partner. Ask each other questions about a story or haiku.

Name _____   Date _____

Strange Garden Plants

Grammar Rules Plural Nouns

1. To make many nouns plural, add -s to the end.

    sprout ➜ sprout<u>s</u>

2. For nouns that end in *x, ch, sh, s, z* and sometimes *o,* add -es.

    branch ➜ branch<u>es</u>   fox ➜ fox<u>es</u>

3. For nouns that end in a consonant plus *y,* change the *y* to *i* and add -es. For nouns that end with a vowel plus *y,* just add -s.

    cherry ➜ cherr<u>ies</u>   boy ➜ boy<u>s</u>

Write the plural nouns.

My grandmother has a strange garden. She has __*boxes*__ full
(box)

of _____ all over her deck. She has _____ of _____
(sprout)   (bunch)   (daisy)

growing in old boots, and _____ in coffee cans. Colored
(lily)

_____ make pretty vases. They line her windowsills. _____
(glass)   (Vine)

curl around her garden swings and _____ . She also made
(bench)

strange metal _____ . She stuck them in the ground between the
(flower)

_____ . Yes, her garden is odd. I love the _____ I spend there.
(bush)   (day)

 Pick two plural nouns from above and write new sentences. Read them to a partner.

Name _____ Date _____

Mark-Up Reading

Grandma's Potato Salad

by Joseph Heinerich

My grandmother's potato salad is the best I've ever eaten. Making it is easy!

1. First, choose four medium potatoes, such as fingerling potatoes. They look like stubby fingers but are very flavorful. Pick ones that fit tightly in your palm.

2. Next, wash and peel the potatoes. Have an adult help you with the peeler.

3. Place the potatoes in a saucepan full of water. Have an adult help you bring the water to a full, bubbling boil.

4. Turn down the heat and boil the potatoes gently for about 15 minutes. The potatoes should be soft but not mushy. You can test if they're done by gently piercing one with a fork. The meaty flesh should be tender.

5. Drain the hot water. Then fill the pan with cold water and set it on the kitchen counter to cool. Then have an adult help you cut the potatoes into quarters or cubes. Place them in a bowl.

6. Next, toss in one-half cup of diced onions and one-half cup of sweet pickle relish. Add one-half cup of creamy mayonnaise. Finally, mix everything together until the mayonnaise coats all the potatoes.

Explanation Step 1: _____

_____

Explanation Steps 3 & 4: _____

_____

Explanation Steps 5 & 6: _____

_____

Name _____ Date _____

Maria's Corn Chowder
by Maria Delgado

Fresh corn chowder is a snap to make. Here are the steps:

1. First, choose four ears of corn. When choosing corn, pull back the husk. The ears should feel firm and solid, and should have plump kernels packed closely together. This means that the kernels have a soft, sweet center.

2. Then melt two tablespoons of butter in a saucepan and blend in one tablespoon of olive oil.

3. Next, add one diced onion, two crushed garlic cloves, and two tablespoons of fresh thyme. Cook for about eight minutes until the vegetables become soft and fragrant. Dust these with one-fourth cup of flour and stir so the flour coats them.

4. Then pour in six cans of vegetable stock and two cups of heavy cream. Also add two peeled, diced baking potatoes.

5. Bring everything to a boil for about seven minutes. While the soup is boiling, have an adult help you cut the corn kernels off the cobs. Then check your boiling soup. The potatoes should be mushy. The broth should be thick and creamy.

6. Now toss in the kernels. Simmer for ten minutes until the corn is spongy. Serve and enjoy.

Explanation Steps 1 & 2: _____

_____

Explanation Steps 3 & 4: _____

_____

Explanation Steps 5 & 6: _____

_____

PM3.14

Edit and Proofread

Choose the Editing and Proofreading Marks you need to correct the passage. Look for the following:

- correct use of singular and plural count nouns
- correct use of punctuation

Editing and Proofreading Marks

∧	Add.
℘	Take out.
∧	Add comma.
∧	Add period.

Joni and Wes Smith moved here from two ~~vallies~~ *valleys* east to start a

new farm. Ralph and Rita Lopez stopped by to welcome them. When

they did the Lopezs were surprised by what they saw. Ralph asked,

"How do you plow your fieldes with donkies instead of tractores?"

Wes explained, "We just like having animales instead of machines."

The two familys sat on benchs in the garden. Rita saw basketes of

fruits. "What are these berrys?" she asked. "Those are actually tiny

tomatos," said Joni.

Then Ralph saw some bushs filled with bright orange pepperes.

"What kind of peppers are those?" he asked. "Very hot ones!" said

Wes. Everyone laughed. When Ralph and Rita left, the Smiths handed

them two boxs of the strange new foods.

Grammar: Reteach

A Golden Crop

Circle the word that completes each sentence.

1. I just ate (bunchs/bunches) of popcorn as a snack.

2. Popcorn is only one of the corn (crops/cropes) grown by farmers.

3. Many tasty (dishs/dishes) around the world are made with corn.

4. The United States ships corn to many (countrys/countries).

5 We grow nearly half of the world's billions of (bushels/busheles).

6. Does it surprise you that about 80% of corn becomes (meales/meals) for animals like pigs and cows?

7. This country grows a lot of (potatos/potatoes) as well.

8. Many (families/familes) enjoy vegetables with their meals.

Name _____ Date _____

Main Idea and Details Diagram

Fill in three details about what makes rainforest plants unusual.

Main Idea:
Rainforest plants are unusual.

Detail 1:

Detail 2:

Detail 3:

 Use your main idea and details diagram to talk to a partner about rainforest plants.

Grammar: Game

It's Special!

Directions:

1. Play with a partner. Copy each word below on a separate card. Place the cards face down and mix them up. Take turns turning over a card.

2. Write the plural form of the noun and use it in a sentence. Some have special forms, and some change spellings.

3. If your partner agrees, keep the card. If your partner disagrees, check the word in a dictionary. Keep the card if you were right. Put it back face down if not.

4. Play until all cards are taken. The player with more cards wins.

berry	Friday	story
chimney	penny	family
cherry	valley	monkey
activity	turkey	dictionary

Grammar: Grammar and Writing

Edit and Proofread

Choose the Editing and Proofreading Marks you need to correct the passage. Look for the following:

- correct use of count nouns with special forms
- use of noncount nouns

Editing and Proofreading Marks

∧	Add.
℘	Take out.

Mr. and Mrs. Snow own a farm. They are looking at Web sites

for vacation ideas. "I want a break from the cold weather," said Mr.

Snow. "It is a chore to chop woods for the fireplace!"

"Plenty of sunshines are important for our vacation," agreed Mrs.

Snow. "Let's go where heats from the sun are strong."

"There's a rainforest preserve in Puerto Rico," said one of their

childs, reading from the computer. "It's about 73 degrees all

the time, and the forest has 240 kinds of trees. Look, it has an

endangered parrot." She thought for a moment. "Oh no, my pet

mouses will be endangered if I leave!"

"All of our sheeps have to be taken care of and farm equipment

need to be put away for the winter," Mrs. Snow said. "Two mans are

doing those chores for us. I think they'll feed your pets."

Name _____   Date _____

Look for Important Words

**Directions: Read each question about "A Protected Place."
Choose the best answer.**

Sample

> **1** Read page 192. What is the paragraph mainly about?
>
> Ⓐ The biggest threat to forests is fire.
>
> Ⓑ People destroy animals' homes.
>
> Ⓒ Ewango works to solve problems.
>
> ● Okapi Reserve still has problems today.

2 Why will the island be a good place for families to live?

Ⓐ Why is Okapi Reserve important?

Ⓑ There was a war.

Ⓒ Houses are made there.

Ⓓ It has a rich diversity of plants and animals.

3 Why are Pygmies called "walking dictionaries of nature?"

Ⓐ They walk to school.

Ⓑ They understand everything about the forest.

Ⓒ The botanists gave them dictionaries.

Ⓓ They carry dictionaries everywhere they go.

 **How did you use the test-taking strategy to answer
the question?**

Main Idea and Details

"A Protected Place"

Make a main idea and details diagram for "A Protected Place."

> **Main Idea:**
> The Okapi Reserve is an amazing place, full of amazing plants.

Supporting Detail:
Supporting Detail:
Supporting Detail:
Supporting Detail:
Supporting Detail:

Fluency Practice

"A Protected Place"

Use this passage to practice reading with proper phrasing.

They understand everything about the forest, and they rely on it	11
for food, shelter, and clothing.	16
Mbuti Pygmies travel from place to place to hunt and fish.	27
They don't just catch game, though.	33
They also collect insects, seeds, fruit, and honey to eat.	43

From "A Protected Place," pages 188-189

Phrasing

1 ☐ Consistent pauses to match appropriate phrasing.   3 ☐ Occasional pauses that match appropriate phrasing.

2 ☐ Frequent pauses that match appropriate phrasing.   4 ☐ Rare pauses at appropriate points in text.

Accuracy and Rate Formula

Use the formula to measure a reader's accuracy and rate while reading aloud.

_____ − _____ = _____
words attempted   number of errors   words correct per minute
in one minute   (wcpm)

Grammar: Reteach

A Day at the Park

Grammar Rules Count and Noncount Nouns

Some **count nouns** use **special forms** to show the plural.	A **man** laughs. My **foot** stomps. My **tooth** aches.	The **men** laugh. My **feet** stomp. My **teeth** ache.
Some **count nouns** use the **same form** for singular and plural.	A **sheep** grazes. A **fish** swims. A **moose** rests.	The **sheep** graze. The **fish** swim. All **moose** rest.
Noncount nouns have only **one form**.	equipment wood	mail corn

Circle the word that completes each sentence.

1. Two (deer / deers) ran along the fence and among the trees.

2. All of the (women / womans) pointed to the running animals.

3. The (childs / children) laughed with delight at the animals.

4. The people sat in the (sunshines / sunshine) and waited quietly.

5. They enjoyed the pleasant (heat / heats) of the afternoon.

6. Everyone thought it would be (funs / fun) if the deer returned.

7. A few people talked about bringing (corns / corn) to feed them.

8. They hoped (mice / mouses) wouldn't eat what they brought.

9. Soon (men / mans) returned from fishing nearby.

10. Families would have a lot of (trouts / trout) for their dinners!

Take a Spin with Your Wheel

Rules

1. One partner spins for a noun. The other partner spins for a verb.

2. Partners work together to write a sentence using the correct form of each word.

3. Spin for a new verb if you can't form a sentence.

4. Take turns spinning for nouns and verbs until you have written 5 sentences.

Noncount Nouns

Verbs

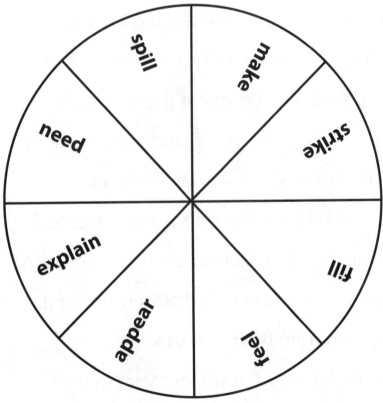

Make a Spinner

1. Put a paper clip in the center of the circle.

2. Put the point of a pencil through the opening of the paper clip at the center of the circle.

3. Spin the paper clip to choose a verb.

4. Use the same steps to choose a noun.

Name _____ Date _____

What Is It?

Directions:

1. Flip a coin. For heads, move ahead 2 squares. For tails, move ahead 1 square.

2. Name the noncount noun that is defined in the square.

3. Use the word in a sentence. If your group agrees that you chose the right word and used it correctly, give yourself one point. If you are incorrect, go back one square.

3. Players take turns moving the game piece. Continue playing until you reach the end. The player with the most points wins.

START   **END**

a rumbling in the sky		mail	corn		You want this to be good, not bad
a flash in the sky	a feeling of joy	water	thunder	breathe it in and out	for ears to enjoy
music	a leafy green vegetable	luck	sand	assigned by a teacher	lightning
homework	a game with a black + white ball	sunshine	soccer	a type of message	lettuce
air	grains on a shore	yellow veggie	a drink for thirst	warm rays	happiness

Name _____ Date _____

Compare Text Features

Compare "A Protected Place" and "Rosie's Reports."

"A Protected Place"	"Rosie's Reports"
Feature: Captions Example: An okapi runs through the woods.	Feature: Captions Example: A worker gets ready to wrap a bundle of leaves.
	Feature: Date line Example: Date: November 8

 Take turns with a partner. Ask each other questions about the blog and the article.

Grammar: Practice

The Make-It-Plural Game

Plural Nouns More Plural Nouns

Add -*s* or -*es* to make most nouns plural:

    plant ➝ plants   box ➝ boxes   baby ➝ babies

For a few nouns, use special forms to show the plural:

    leaf ➝ leaves   foot ➝ feet   man ➝ men

    woman ➝ women   child ➝ children

1. **Play with a partner.**

2. **Spin the spinner.**

3. **Change the noun to a plural noun. Say a sentence using the plural noun.**

Make a Spinner

1. Push a brad 🝙 through the center of the spinner.
2. Open the brad on the back.
3. Hook a paper clip ⊂══⊃ over the brad on the front to make a spinner.

party

leaf

woman

fork

foot

fox

child

flower

Name _____ Date _____

Let's **Protect** the **Okapi Reserve!**
by Emeka Obadina

Thousands of animals roam freely in the Okapi Wildlife Reserve in the Ituri Forest. But this important reserve is in danger. Find out how to protect it!

1. Learn More About the Reserve

The more you learn, the more you can do to help protect the reserve. More than 1,500 species of plants and animals live only in the Ituri Forest. The Okapi Wildlife Reserve protects many of these threatened plants and animals, including the okapi. Follow this Web link to learn more about this unique animal and its home: Okapi Video: "Rare Breed".

2. Understand the Problems

Some methods of local farmers harm the reserve. Farmers clear land by cutting down and burning the rainforest. This damages the soil. After a few years, the soil becomes unusable, and farmers must move on to new parts of the forest. Unfortunately, when a part of the forest is destroyed, it can never grow back!

▲ Ituri Forest

▲ Farmers cut and burn trees.

Explanation: _____
_____
_____
_____

Name _____ Date _____

Let's **Protect** the **Okapi Reserve!** (continued)

3. Learn About the Okapi Conservation Project (OCP)

The Okapi Conservation Project works with local communities. It focuses on young people, who may grow up to become farmers and scientists. The OCP shares easy ways to protect the rainforest.

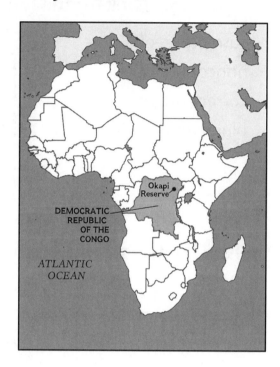

The OCP also provides jobs to local people as guards. The guards have the toughest job. They have to protect animals from illegal hunting. They also have to stop people from cutting down trees and harming the forest. The guards help show their communities how to protect the reserve.

4. Raise Awareness

Spread the news about what you learned.

- Talk to others about the reserve and OCP's tireless efforts to protect it.

- Work with your school to hold a fundraiser. Make informative and colorful posters for the event.

- E-mail organizations, such as OCP, to ask how you and your school can help.

Explanation: _____

_____

_____

_____

Grammar: Grammar and Writing

Edit and Proofread

Choose the Editing and Proofreading Marks you need to correct the passage. Look for the following:

- correct use of noncount nouns
- correct use of plural nouns

Editing and Proofreading Marks

∧	Add.
ی	Take out.
⋏	Add comma.
⋏	Add period.

I am the tallest living animal. When I was born, I was six ~~foots~~ *feet* tall. As an adult, I am about 14 to 18 foots tall with a very long neck. I have a creamy coat with brown or black splotchs. What am I!

I am a giraffe! Giraffes share the dry land with elephants, lions, zebras, and antelopes—but not with sheeps or deers. There aren't a lot of waters here, but we can go a long time without drinking.

We eat grasss, fruites, shrubs, and a lot of juicy leaves from acacia trees. We don't need any helps from a ladder to get leaves on top! Acacias have long thorns on them, but we have longer tongues. Our tongues are 18 inchs long. Thorns don't stop us!

We have heavy bodys that weigh from 1,500 to 3,000 poundes. Even so, we can run as fast as 30-35 miles per hour!

Name _____ Date _____

Meals for Good Health

Grammar Rules Plural Nouns

Count Nouns

- Add -s or -es to make most nouns plural.

- Change y to i and add -es when a consonant comes before the y.

- For a few nouns, use special forms to show the plural.

vegetable → vegetable*s*	
dish → dish*es*	
tomato → tomato*es*	
strawberry → strawberr*ies*	
tooth → teeth	

Noncount Nouns

- Use the same form to name "one" and "more than one."

water → water
lettuce → lettuce

Write the correct form of the noun to complete each sentence.

1. Many _____ were at the restaurant when we arrived.
   (family)

2. Two giggling _____ were being put into highchairs.
   (child)

3. The chef had planned several yummy _____ .
   (recipe)

4. We heard many _____ of her voice in the kitchen.
   (echo)

5. The kitchen sounded busy as they made many _____ .
   (lunch)

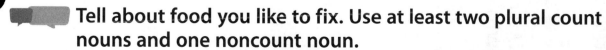 **Tell about food you like to fix. Use at least two plural count nouns and one noncount noun.**

Unit Concept Map

Let's Work Together

Make a concept map with the answers to the Big Question:
What's the best way to get things done?

What's the best way to get things done?

Name _____ Date _____

Story Clues

Make a theme chart about your partner's story.

Title: _____

Clues from the Title:	Clues from the Characters:
Clues from the Setting:	Clues from the Events:

Theme:

 Discuss the clues in the theme chart with a partner.

Grammar: Game

Everyone Is Present

Directions:

1. Make two pronoun cards for each pronoun: *he, she,* and *it.*

2. Shuffle the six cards and stack them face down.

3. Take turns drawing a card and tossing a marker onto a square.

4. Form a sentence using the word from the card and the verb your marker lands on. Write a sentence using the pronoun and the verb. For example: "It stretches."

5. Award yourself one point for using the correct present tense of the verb and one point for spelling it correctly.

6. Put the pronoun card at the bottom of the stack.

7. After eight turns each, the player with more points wins.

hum	fetch	gather
leave	wave	tap
miss	rush	cheer
skip	chase	stretch
pour	visit	mix

Edit and Proofread

Choose the Editing and Proofreading Marks you need to correct the passage. Look for correct usage of the following:

- present-tense action verbs
- subject-verb agreement with *he*, *she*, and *it*

Editing and Proofreading Marks

∧	Add.
و	Take out.
≡	Capitalize.
⊙	Add period.
⋏	Add comma.

    Mimi finish^es cutting the strawberries. She places them into a bowl. She smile as she leaves the kitchen. Everything is ready, and neighbors will arrive soon.

    Suddenly, Mimi hear a crash and rushs into the kitchen. It was the cat! She see the bowl of strawberries on the floor.

    When Jeff gets home, Mimi discuss the problem with him. They have no dessert! Then Mimi's phone buzz. It's their neighbor, Mrs. Wong. She want to know what to bring. "Bring strawberries!" say Mimi.

    Mimi smiles again. "That fix our dessert problem," she says.

Test-Taking Strategy Practice

Understand the Question

**Directions: Read each question about "Mama Panya's Pancakes."
Choose the best answer.**

Sample

> **1** How does Mama feel when Adika invites several guests to
> have pancakes?
>
> ● nervous
>
> Ⓑ excited
>
> Ⓒ sad

2 Which answer best shows that Adika is generous?

Ⓐ He is always one step ahead of Mama Panya.

Ⓑ He invites people over to eat pancakes.

Ⓒ He is friendly to everyone he meets.

3 Why does Kaya give Mama Panya the plumpest pepper?

Ⓐ Adika invites her for pancakes.

Ⓑ Kaya and Mama Panya are friends.

Ⓒ Kaya is a generous person.

4 Choose the statement that best fits the theme of being generous.

Ⓐ "Aiii! How many pancakes do you think I can make today, son?"

Ⓑ "I think we can give you a little more for that coin."

Ⓒ "You and I will be lucky to share half a pancake."

**How did you use the test-taking strategy to answer
the questions?**

Name _____ Date _____

"Mama Panya's Pancakes"

Make a theme chart for "Mama Panya's Pancakes."

Theme Chart

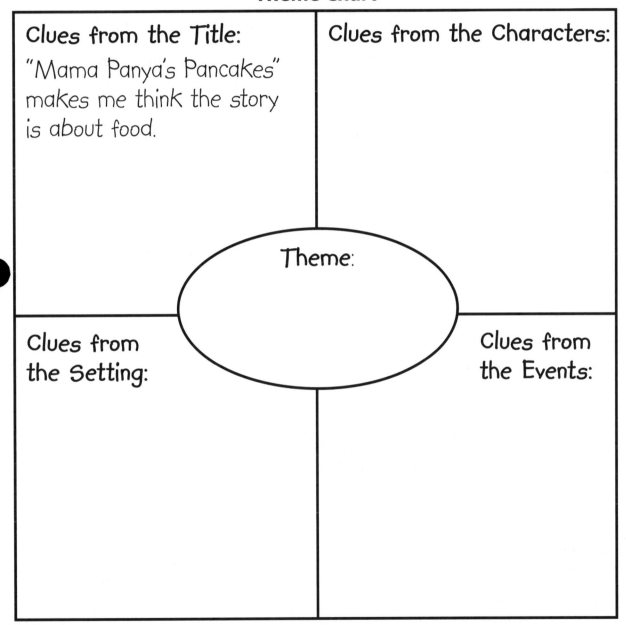

Clues from the Title:

"Mama Panya's Pancakes" makes me think the story is about food.

Clues from the Characters:

Theme:

Clues from the Setting:

Clues from the Events:

 Compare your theme sentence with a partner's sentence. Can both themes apply to the story? Discuss.

Fluency Practice

"Mama Panya's Pancakes"

Use this passage to practice reading with proper intonation.

Adika popped up. "Mama's making pancakes today. Can you come?"   10

"Oh, how wonderful! I think we can give a little more for that coin."   24

Bwana Zawenna put more flour on the paper, then tied it up with string.   38

"We'll see you later."   42

Mama tucked the package into her bag. "Ai-Yi-Yi! You and I will be   55

lucky to share half a pancake."   61

"But Mama, we have a little bit and a little bit more."   73

From "Mama Panya's Pancakes," page 226

Intonation

| 1 | ☐ Does not change pitch. | 3 | ☐ Changes pitch to match some of the content. |
| 2 | ☐ Changes pitch, but does not match content. | 4 | ☐ Changes pitch to match all of the content. |

Accuracy and Rate Formula
Use the formula to measure a reader's accuracy and rate while reading aloud.

$$\underline{\hspace{3cm}} - \underline{\hspace{3cm}} = \underline{\hspace{3cm}}$$

| words attempted in one minute | number of errors | words correct per minute (wcpm) |

Grammar: Reteach

A Fair Trade

Grammar Rules Subject-Verb Agreement with Present Tense

A **present-tense action verb** tells about an action that happens now or all the time.	The baker **reads** the recipe.
	"It **lists** cinnamon!" he **yells** to an assistant.
To show present tense for the subject **he**, **she**, or **it**, add -**s** or -**es** to most action verbs.	She **adds** cinnamon to the bowl.
	He **mixes** the bread dough.
	It bakes in the oven.

Circle the present-tense verb that completes each sentence.

1. A girl sits near the bakery. She (sniff/sniffs) the cinnamon scent.

2. The baker stomps up to her. He (glares/glare) at the young girl.

3. Then he (demand/demands), "You pay for enjoying the scent!"

4. The girl says, "It smells wonderful!" She (find/finds) her only coin.

5. She (tosses/toss) the coin, and it (sparkles/sparkle) in the light.

6. He (catches/catch) the coin and (twirl/twirls) it happily.

7. Then he (flip/flips) it high in the air, and the girl grabs the coin.

8. The baker says, "It belongs to me!" and he (step/steps) closer.

9. "I smelled the cinnamon. You felt the coin." The girl (grin/grins).

10. The baker frowns. Suddenly, he (flashes/flash) a smile. "It *is* a fair trade."

 Tell a partner about an event or a trade that is fair. Include present-tense action verbs, and use *he*, *she*, and *it*.

Grammar: Game

Apply the -y Rules

Directions:

1. Choose a game box that has not been filled in.

A.B. **scurry**
scurries

2. Use the correct present tense of the verb in a sentence with *he*, *she*, or *it*. Then spell the verb aloud.

3. If other players agree with the spelling, write the word and your initials in the box. If the spelling is wrong, leave the box blank.

4. Players take turns. When all boxes are taken, count your boxes. The player with the most boxes is the winner.

try	say	study
_____	_____	_____
rely	pay	buy
_____	_____	_____
bury	cry	carry
_____	_____	_____
annoy	play	fly
_____	_____	_____
stay	hurry	employ
_____	_____	_____

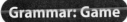

Grammar: Game

Do They Agree?

Directions:

1. Flip a coin. For heads, move 2 squares. For tails, move 1 square.

2. Pick a SUBJECT card and read it aloud. Choose the correct present-tense verb in the square to create a sentence with your subject. Then put the SUBJECT card at the bottom of the stack.

3. If the other players agree that your subject and verb agree, stay on your space. If not, move back one space.

> **SUBJECT Cards**
> 1. Print I, YOU, WE, THEY, HE, SHE, IT on separate index cards.
> 2. Mix the SUBJECT cards up and stack them face down to play the game.

					dash or dashes? **END**
	explore or explores?	trades or trade?	raise or raises?		study or studies?
	scurries or scurry?		pay or pays?		hides or hide?
	works or work?		buys or buy?		finds or find?
hurries or hurry?	help or helps?		move or moves?	sells or sell?	buzz or buzzes?
START go or goes?					

Name _____ Date _____

Compare Characters

Compare the characters from the two stories.

	Beginning of Story	End of Story	Why does the character change?
Mama Payna	She is worried about having enough food.		
Ba			

 Talk with a partner about which story you liked better and why.

Name _____   Date _____

Farmer's Market

Grammar Rules Present-Tense Action Verbs

A present-tense action verb must agree with its subject.

Use **-s** at the end of an action verb if the subject is *he*, *she*, or *it*.	Carmella **loves** street fairs. She **takes** me along with her.
Do **not** add -s to the verb if the subject is *I*, *you*, *we*, or *they*.	Buyers **walk** slowly through the fairs. They **buy** a lot of things.

Fill in each blank with the present-tense verb form that agrees with the subject.

My parents _____ us to the farmer's market. We _____
           (take)   (enjoy)
all the sights, smells, and sounds. Farmers _____ vegetables
                                              (sell)
and fruit. One farmer _____ flowers, too. My mother _____
                            (sell)   (buy)
flowers every week. She _____ flowers. One man _____
                              (love)   (cook)
delicious burritos. A woman _____ faces. Two men _____
                               (paint)   (carve)
wooden toys. They _____ out to buyers. The farmer's market is
                           (call)
so much fun! It _____ me smile.
                  (make)

 Choose three verbs from the story and write new sentences. Read them to a partner.

PM4.12

The Bird Bank by Grace Lin

During the winter, Hannah and Rose earned nickels from their father. Sometimes they would shovel snow or sweep the house. Ba would give them each a nickel and they put the nickels in their green bird bank.

Every time Hannah and Rose put their nickels in the bird bank it would sing "Tweet! Tweet!"

But in the spring, the bird bank stopped singing. It would not swallow Rose's nickel.

"Hannah!" Rose said. "Our bird bank is full!"

Shopping by Grace Lin

Hannah and Rose looked at all the stores. What should they buy?

"Look at the birds!" Rose said, pointing at a pet store window. "I like the yellow one."

"I like the blue one," Hannah said. "Let's go buy them!"

But Hannah and Rose did not have enough money for a yellow bird or a blue bird. On the shelf there was a birdhouse.

"We can buy the birdhouse," Rose said. "Should we buy that instead?"

Hannah nodded and they did.

Name _____ Date _____

Tweet! Tweet! by Grace Lin

Hannah and Rose bought the birdhouse at the pet store.

"I'm glad you are buying a birdhouse," Mrs. Alexis, the store owner, said. "I have too many of them. No one else is buying them. I wonder why." She sighed sadly.

Hannah and Rose brought their birdhouse home.

"This is a nice birdhouse," Rose said to Hannah, "but it is too plain. Let's decorate it."

So, Hannah painted the birdhouse and Rose glued on pictures. When they were finished, the birdhouse was very pretty.

"I know why no one else is buying Mrs. Alexis's birdhouses," Rose said. "They are too plain! They need to be decorated."

"We should tell her," Hannah said. "Let's show her our birdhouse."

When Mrs. Alexis saw Hannah and Rose's decorated birdhouse, she was surprised.

"Could you decorate all of my birdhouses?" she said. "I will pay you for every birdhouse that sells."

So, Hannah and Rose decorated the other birdhouses. How pretty they were! Soon, many people began to buy them. Mrs. Alexis paid Hannah and Rose for their good work and was very happy.

Hannah and Rose put their new quarters and dimes into their bird bank. Two live birds came to live in their birdhouse. All of them sang "Tweet! Tweet!" for Hannah and Rose.

Compare Story Elements

For each story, list the characters, settings, and story events found only in that story. Then list elements found in multiple stories.

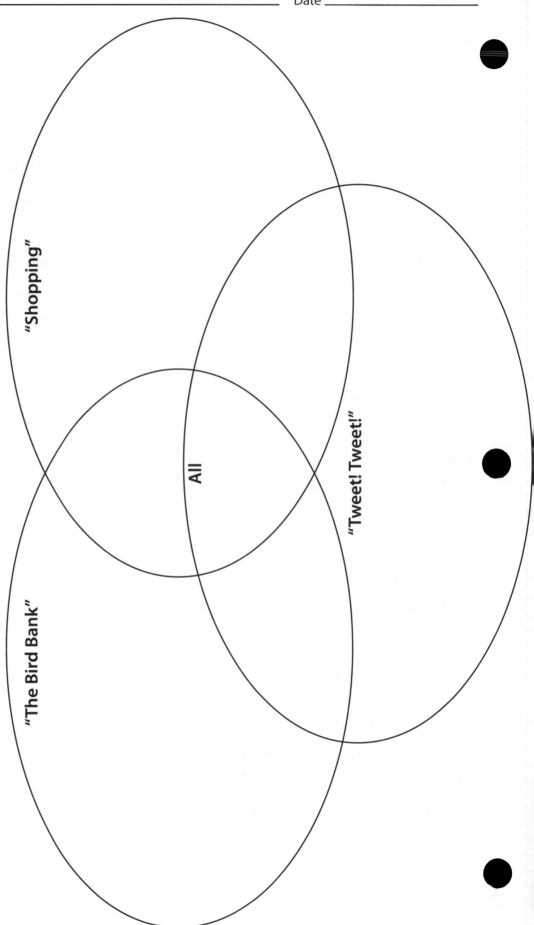

"Shopping"

"The Bird Bank"

All

"Tweet! Tweet!"

PM4.15

Edit and Proofread

Choose the Editing and Proofreading Marks you need to correct the passage. Look for correct usage of the following:

- present-tense action verbs
- subject-verb agreement
- correct spelling of verbs

Editing and Proofreading Marks

∧	Add.
ℐ	Take out.
≡	Capitalize.
⊙	Add period.

"Have you finished the patchwork quilt?" Lee asks Kendra.

"No," she replies holding it up. "It won't be ready for Mama's

birthday. It need another row, but I ran out of material."

"If you requires material, I'll get it," Lee promises. He dashs out.

Neighbors help, but they adds only a few scraps to his bag. He go

to Ms. Cotton. She explains, "I buys material for my store! Here, you

carries these back to Kendra."

When Kendra sees the cloth, she exclaim, "Look at this special

piece, Lee. It shine like a pool of water!" Kendra tells Lee, "Now the

quilt can be ready! We makes a good team, brother!"

Name _____ Date _____

Pet Show

Grammar Rules Subject-Verb Agreement

Present-Tense Action Verbs

Singular subject: Use -**s** or -**es** if the subject is **he**, **she**, or **it**.	He <u>pats</u> his big dog. It <u>swishes</u> its long, fluffy tail. She <u>hurries</u> to the pet show.
Plural subject: Do <u>not</u> use -s or -es at the end of an action verb if the subject is **we**, **you**, or **they.**	We <u>help</u> the judges. You <u>watch</u> the time for us. They <u>walk</u> around each pet.
Exceptions: For singular subjects **I** and **you**, do <u>not</u> use -s or -es.	I <u>take</u> a video of the contest. You <u>bring</u> the prize ribbons.

Read each sentence. Write the correct form of the verb on the line.

1. Owners hold leashes and cages. They _____ eagerly.
   (smile)

2. Judges have a hard job. "We _____ to be fair to all pets."
   (promise)

3. A judge holds a gerbil. "He _____ in his wheel," says the boy.
   (race)

4. "I _____ great!" A judge laughs because the speaker is a parrot.
   (sing)

5. She _____ the parrot. It _____ for a treat after singing.
   (study)   (reach)

6. Another judge says, "You _____ your dogs to the ring."
   (lead)

Name _____ Date _____

For use with TE p. T241a

PM4.18

Opinion Chart

What Do You Think?

Make an opinion chart of your partner's opinion.

Opinion:

Evidence:

Evidence:

Evidence:

Ask your partner questions about his or her opinion.

Name _____ Date _____

Could You? You Can!

Helping Verbs: What They Mean	
The helping verb **can** means • someone is able to do something • someone knows how to do something • someone has the power to do something.	The helping verb **could** means • someone has a choice • something is possible • a suggestion is being offered.

Directions:

1. Write **can** on five cards and **could** on five cards. Mix the cards and place them face down.

2. Take turns spinning for a main verb and choosing a card for the helping verb.

3. Use the main verb and helping verb in a sentence.

4. When each player has created five correct sentences, work together to write a three-sentence story. Use helping verbs and main verbs. Share your story.

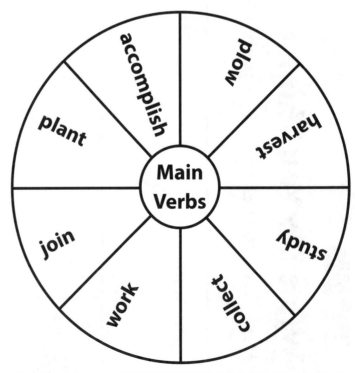

Make a Spinner

1. Put a paper clip over the center of the spinner.
2. Touch the point of a pencil on the middle of the wheel and through the loop of the paper clip.
3. Spin the paper clip to make a spinner.

Grammar: Grammar and Writing

Edit and Proofread

Choose the Editing and Proofreading Marks you need to correct the passage. Look for correct usage of the following:

- helping verbs *can, could, must, should, do*

Editing and Proofreading Marks

∧	Add.
ℐ	Take out.
≡	Capitalize.
⊙	Add period.
⅄	Add comma.

We know forests are important to the planet. People ~~might~~ stop *(must)*

slash-and-burn farming. We don't want more forests to disappear.

Farmers have choices. They must harvest plants like orchids, or

harvest fruit from trees. Some farmers have already changed their

methods. They does harvest Brazil nuts, palm hearts, and other foods.

They agree that more farmers do change their crops.

Education helps farmers work faster and better. They learn that

they could grow or harvest crops without cutting down trees.

We know how important good farming is. It do make a difference

to the planet.

Name _____ Date _____

Understand the Question

Directions: Read each question about "A Better Way."
Choose the best answer.

Sample

1 Why is sustainable agriculture a good alternative to the
slash-and-burn method of farming?

- ● Sustainable agriculture allows people to reuse the land.
- Ⓑ Slash-and-burn farming is too expensive for many farmers.
- Ⓒ Slash-and-burn farming only grows certain crops.
- Ⓓ Sustainable agriculture takes less time.

2 Segura and Simões believe that we need to save trees and help
people, too. Which statement does not support their opinion?

- Ⓐ Fruit and flower trees can provide a good income.
- Ⓑ Sustainable agriculture is good for the land.
- Ⓒ Farmers can grow high-value crops.
- Ⓓ Slash-and-burn agriculture harms the land and people.

3 What is the name of Segura and Simões' alternative farming plan?

- Ⓐ Slash-and-burn agriculture
- Ⓑ Fruit-and-flower agriculture
- Ⓒ A special plan
- Ⓓ The 5 X 5 System

 **How did you use the test-taking strategy to answer
the question?**

Name _____ Date _____

"A Better Way"

Make an opinion chart for pages 254-257 in "A Better Way."

Opinion: Sustainable agriculture is good for the farmer and good for the land.

Evidence: It lets farmers grow crops on the same land year after year.

Evidence:

Evidence:

 Explain the opinion and evidence to a partner.

For use with TE p. T258a   **PM4.22**   **Unit 4** | Let's Work Together

"A Better Way"

Use this passage to practice reading with proper phrasing.

To make a difference, many farmers need to grow crops this way.	12
Segura and Simões use a special plan to teach more farmers. It is	25
called the 5 x 5 System. First, they teach one family how to grow	39
crops that don't ruin the land. Then that family teaches five new	51
families what they learned. Each new family teaches five more	61
families. Think of all the land that could be saved in the future!	74

From "A Better Way," page 253

Phrasing

1 ☐ Rarely pauses while reading the text.

2 ☐ Occasionally pauses while reading the text.

3 ☐ Frequently pauses at appropriate points in the text.

4 ☐ Consistently pauses at all appropriate points in the text.

Accuracy and Rate Formula
Use the formula to measure a reader's accuracy and rate while reading aloud.

$$\underline{\hspace{2cm}} - \underline{\hspace{2cm}} = \underline{\hspace{2cm}}$$

| words attempted in one minute | number of errors | words correct per minute (wcpm) |

Name _____ Date _____

Traveling Straight Up

Grammar Rules Helping Verbs

A **helping verb** works with the <u>main verb</u> to tell something about the action.

- Use **can** to tell that someone is able to do something.
- Use **could** to tell that someone has a choice or something is possible.
- Use **must** to tell that somebody has to do something.
- Use **should** to give an opinion or advice about doing something.
- Use **do** to add emphasis to a verb.

People **can** <u>see</u> skyscrapers in big cities.

You **could** <u>visit</u> New York City to see some.

People **must** <u>use</u> elevators in skyscrapers.

You **should** <u>visit</u>.

I **do** <u>ride</u> in a glass elevator!

It **does** <u>go</u> fast!

Read each sentence. Write the correct form of the verb on the line.

1. This is advice:

They _____ go to the Empire State Building.

2. They are able:

They _____ reach the 102nd floor of the building.

3. You have to do this:

You _____ see the view across the city from there!

4. This is a choice.

You _____ stop at the 86th floor.

 Tell a partner if he or she should ride elevators to reach the 102nd floor. Use three helping verbs.

Be What You Want to Be

Directions:

1. Take five minutes to write as many sentences as your team can. For each sentence, use a subject from column 1, the correct form of *to be*, and a word or phrase from column 2.

2. Your team will get one point for each sentence it writes correctly.

3. You may choose one or all subjects in a box to use in sentences. For example, if you write one correct sentence with *he*, another with *she*, and another with *it*, you gain three points! You can also use words in column 2 more than once.

4. When time's up, trade sentences with another team, check each other's work, and add up points. The team with most points wins.

Forms of *To Be*		
am	is	are

Subject	What the Subject Is or What the Subject is Like
I	challenging
He, She, It	a hard worker
You	curious
We, They	busy
Problems	thoughtful
An ant | Ants	delicious
A grasshopper	nine years old
A kernel | Kernels	playful
An inventor | Inventors	bright yellow
An invention | Inventions	a problem solver

Name _____ Date _____

Choose *Has* or *Have*

Directions:

1. Play with a partner. Take turns.

2. Place a game piece on START. Flip a coin. For heads, move ahead one space. For tails, move ahead two spaces.

3. Read the subject in the space. Create a sentence using the subject and the verb *has* or *have* to tell what the subject has. Or, use the verb *has* or *have* as a helping verb in a sentence. If your partner agrees that your sentence is correct, score one point.

4. When one player reaches the END, count your points to see who wins.

have	has	START	have	has	have	has	have	has
has		I						have
have		Paola						has
has		he	she	you	Ba	we		have
have		friends	I			it		has
has		it	they			Cid		have
have		we	you			they		has
has	have	has	have	has	have	END	has	have

Name _____ Date _____

Compare Purposes

Compare authors' purposes in "A Better Way" and "The Ant and the Grasshopper."

Title	Topic	Author's Purpose
"A Better Way" by Juan Quintana	sustainable agriculture	
"The Ant and the Grasshopper" by Shirleyann Costigan		

Take turns with a partner telling how the authors' purposes are alike or different.

PM4.27

Name _____ Date _____

What Is in the Garden?

Grammar Rules Subject-Verb Agreement: *be* and *have*

The verbs *be* and *have* are irregular. The subject and verb must agree. Use these correct forms:

I am	We are	I have	We have
You are	You are	You have	You have
He, she, it is	They are	He, she, it has	They have

Write the correct form of be or have to complete each sentence. Choose the correct form for the subject.

Jenna and Jake ___have___ a large garden. Jake's favorite

vegetable _____ corn. He _____ several rows of corn in the

garden. The corn _____ almost ready to harvest. Both Jenna

and Jake _____ excited to roast ears of corn. They also grow

tomatoes. Tomatoes _____ their mother's favorite vegetable.

Jenna planted sunflowers, too. They _____ delicious seeds and

pretty blooms.

I _____ planning to help them pick some corn. I _____ a

basket I will take with me.

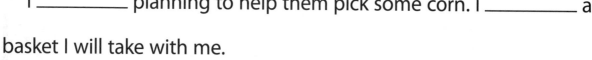 **Imagine a garden. Tell your partner about it, using forms of** *be* **and** *have*.

Mark-Up Reading

Belling the Cat

an Aesop fable retold by Katie Blankshain

Long ago, a large family of mice lived in an old blue house. They chattered happily that they had all the food and warmth they could ever need. There was just one problem. They worried that their enemy the cat was becoming more dangerous every day.

Every day, the cat would tiptoe through the gray shadows, stepping lightly with her furry feet. She would slink and creep, grinning to herself as she went. She waited until she was right behind the poor mice. Then—POUNCE—she would trap one of the mice in her big orange paws. "You'll make a delicious dinner for me tonight!" the cat would say, purring.

Her cruel trick never failed, and so the cat never went hungry. She began to grow quite fat and content. Sometimes she would pop out from behind corners, baring her white, pointy teeth and sharp claws, just to scare the helpless mice away.

Explain these viewpoints:

1. the mice _____
_____

2. the cat _____
_____

3. the narrator _____
_____

Mark-Up Reading

Belling the Cat (continued)

One night, the oldest mouse called a meeting. "Fellow mice!" he cried. "We have lived in fear of the cat for too long. She must be stopped. Who has a plan? We might be smaller than the cat, but surely we can outwit her."

Everyone was silent for a long while. At last, a young mouse stood up. "The cat only catches us because she is very sneaky. If we knew when cat was coming, we could certainly run away in time." The small mouse held up a large red collar. "Here is my plan: we should attach a small bell to the cat using this collar. This way, the bell will ring whenever the cat moves. She will never sneak up on us again!" All of the mice joyfully applauded this idea.

Then an old mouse slowly rose to his feet. "That is a good idea, but who is to put the bell on the cat?" All of the mice looked around, but no one spoke. No mouse wanted to volunteer for such a dangerous mission.

MORAL: Actions speak louder than words.

Explain these viewpoints:

1. the mice _____

_____

_____

2. the narrator _____

_____

_____

Name _____ Date _____

Edit and Proofread

Choose the Editing and Proofreading Marks you need to correct the passage. Look for correct usage of the following:

- subject-verb agreement with forms of *be*
- subject-verb agreement with forms of *have*

Editing and Proofreading Marks

∧	Add.
℘	Take out.
≡	Capitalize.
⊙	Add period.
∧.	Add comma.

Ella Ant ~~are~~ is unhappy. She is on one side of some flowing water.

Tempting smells come from the other side. "I is hungry, but I are not a

swimmer," she says. She have no boat.

"Ants is clever," thinks Ella. "We has problem-solving skills." She

looks around. "Ah, leaves is good boats. They has the ability to float."

She invents a two-leaf boat to carry back food. She pushes it into the

water, but it quickly floats away.

Grasshopper hops into view. "You am eager to be on the other side,

I see," he says. "I has a solution for you."

With Ella on his back, Grasshopper leaps across the water. Together

they follow the tempting smells.

Name _____ Date _____

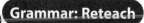

The Science Museum

Grammar Rules Forms of *Be* and *Have*

• The linking verb **to be** tells what a subject is or is like.	I **am**	we **are**
	you **are**	you **are**
• The verb **to be** has irregular forms.	she, he, it **is**	they **are**
• The verb **to have** can tell what the subject of a sentence has.	I **have**	we **have**
	you **have**	you **have**
• The verb **to have** has irregular forms.	she, he, it **has**	they **have**

Read each sentence. Write the correct verb from the box. Then read your sentences again to make sure the subjects and verbs agree.

am	is	are	has	have

1. This science museum _____ many exciting inventions.

2. The can opener _____ one of the most practical ones.

3. Science certainly _____ come a long way!

4. Inventions _____ changed our lives.

5. Our lives _____ easier because of them.

6. Inventions _____ created by clever people.

7. I _____ hoping someday to invent something.

8. Jenna says she _____ going to invent something, too.

 Tell a partner what inventions you think are interesting. Use at least one *be* verb and one *have* verb.

Unit Concept Map

States of Matter

Make a concept map with the answers to the Big Question:
What causes matter to change?

What causes matter to change?

Name _____ Date _____

Partner Skit

Make a character-plot chart about your skit.

Character	What the Character Says	What This Shows About the Character	What This Shows About the Plot

 Take turns telling a partner about one of the characters. What do the character's words show about the character?

Grammar: Game

Rising Temperatures

Directions:

1. Write your names below the thermometer.

2. Take turns choosing an adjective from the Adjectives box.

3. Use -*est* or *most* to say the correct form of the adjective for comparing three or more things. Then use it in a sentence with a noun from the Helpful Nouns box.

4. If your partner agrees the form is correct, put a checkmark beside the word and write the correct form in the first empty space above your name. Color the thermometer next to your adjective.

5. The player who reaches the END in fewer turns wins.

Adjectives	
___ warm	___ bright
___ beautiful	___ strong
___ powerful	___ exciting
___ gray	___ unusual
___ cold	___ dark

Helpful Nouns		
weather	day	summer
snow	clouds	fall
storm	week	blizzard
wind	month	rain
spring	fog	winter
year	sun	night

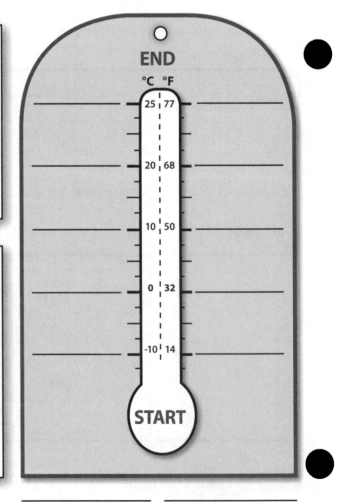

_____   _____
Name   Name

Grammar: Grammar and Writing

Edit and Proofread

Choose the Editing and Proofreading Marks you need to correct the passage. Look for correct usage of the following:

- adjectives that describe
- adjectives that compare two things
- adjectives that compare three or more things

Editing and Proofreading Marks

∧	Add.
ꝑ	Take out.
≡	Capitalize.
⊙	Add period.
∧̣	Add comma.

"It is ~~more~~ colder tonight than it was today," Hormiguita says

sadly. "Listen to that howling wind!" She pulls on a greener sweater.

"This winter has the low temperatures in many years," Mami says.

She picks the colorfulest yarn from a basket full of knitting. Before

starting to knit, she looks outside. She sees a grayer mouse blown

like a tumbleweed by the wind. "Hormiguita, is that your friend?"

"Oh, poorest Mouse!" Hormiguita cries. Mami opens the door

against the dangerousest wind of all. "Mouse, come in!"

Mouse rushes in. "You are oldest than Hormiguita," says Mouse,

"so you must be Mami. I am the oldest one here, and this is the

amazingest kindness I've seen in my life!" Mouse hugs them both.

Reread

Directions: Read each question about *Melt the Snow!* Choose the best answer.

Sample

1 Who is stronger than Snow?
- Ⓐ Cloud
- ● Sun
- Ⓒ Wind
- Ⓓ Hormiguita

2 How is Cloud stronger than Sun?
- Ⓐ Cloud covers Sun's warm rays.
- Ⓑ Cloud rains on Sun's warm rays.
- Ⓒ Cloud uncovers Sun's warm rays.
- Ⓓ Cloud snows on Sun's warm rays.

3 Who is stronger than Wind?
- Ⓐ Snow
- Ⓑ Mami
- Ⓒ Sun
- Ⓓ Wall

4 What does Mami make for Hormiguita when she returns home?
- Ⓐ dinner
- Ⓑ a hot bath
- Ⓒ hot chocolate
- Ⓓ a snowstorm

 How did you use the test-taking strategy to answer the questions?

Character-Plot Chart

Melt the Snow!

Make a character-plot chart for *Melt the Snow!*

Character	What the Character Says	What This Shows About the Character	What This Shows About the Plot
Mami	"Don't go far, and be very careful."	Mami wants Hormiguita to be safe.	Mami lets Hormiguita go out to play.
Hormiguita			

 How does the play's dialogue help you understand its characters and plot? Use your character-plot chart to explain this to a partner.

Fluency Practice

Melt the Snow!

Use this passage to practice reading with proper expression.

HORMIGUITA [*pointing*]: *¡Mami, mira!* Look,	3
the sun is shining. It's melting the snow.	11
It's been such a long winter, and I'm tired of	21
staying indoors. May I go out and play?	29

From *Melt the Snow!* page 284

Fluency: Expression

1 ☐ Does not read with feeling.

2 ☐ Reads with some feeling, but does not match content.

3 ☐ Reads with appropriate feeling for most content.

4 ☐ Reads with appropriate feeling for all content.

Accuracy and Rate Formula

Use the formula to measure a reader's accuracy and rate while reading aloud.

$$\underline{\hspace{3cm}} - \underline{\hspace{3cm}} = \underline{\hspace{3cm}}$$

| words attempted in one minute | number of errors | words correct per minute (wcpm) |

Name _____ Date _____

Let It Snow

Grammar Rules Comparison Adjectives

• An **adjective** describes, or tells about, a noun.	A **light** snow fell on the **busy** city.
• Add **-er** followed by **than** to compare two things. • If the adjective has three or more syllables, use **more** followed by **than**.	The snow in the country was deep**er than** in the city. An icy road is **more** dangerous **than** a dry road.
• Add **-est** to compare three or more things. Use **the** in front of the adjective. • If the adjective has three or more syllables, use **the most**.	A snowy day with sunshine is **the** bright**est** day of all. A snowy woods is **the most** wonderful of all places.

Read each sentence. Write the correct form of the comparison adjective on the line.

1. We have _____ paw prints in our snowy yard.
    (strange)

2. Prints in the park are _____ than those in our yard.
    (interesting)

3. _____ prints of all are in the woods.
    (mysterious)

4. Birds, mice, and moles leave the _____ of all footprints.
    (small)

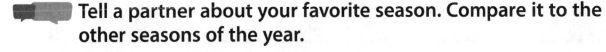 **Tell a partner about your favorite season. Compare it to the other seasons of the year.**

Grammar: Game

Let's Compare!

Directions:

1. Take turns. Flip a coin. For heads, move 2 squares. For tails, move 1 square.

2. Follow the directions in the square. Use one of the gray adjectives in your description.

   Remember: To describe one thing, use **good** or **bad**. To compare two things, use **better** or **worse**. To compare three or more things, use **best** or **worst**.

3. If the group agrees that you have used the gray adjective correctly, stay on your space. If not, move back one space. The player who reaches the end first wins.

Good	Better	Bad	Best	Worst	Compare 3 or more pets.	END
Best	Compare 3 or more foods.	Compare 2 classes.	Compare 3 or more classes.	Better	Compare 2 pets.	
Better	Describe 1 food.	Worse	Describe 1 class.	Best	Compare 3 or more pairs of shoes.	
Worst	Compare 2 meals.	Better	Describe 1 bike.	Worse	Describe 1 pair of shoes.	
Compare 2 days.	Compare 3 or more days.	Good	Compare 2 bikes	Compare 3 or more bikes.	Compare 2 pairs of shoes.	
START	Describe 1 day.	Worse	Bad	Better	Good	Best

Grammar: Game

Good or Bad?

Directions:

1. Copy the phrases at bottom, cut them into cards, and stack them face down.

2. Take turns. Spin the spinner. Then choose a card.

3. Follow the directions on the card to make a sentence. Use the correct form of the adjective on the spinner. For example, if you land on "bad" and draw "Compare three or more things," you could say, "The Ice Age had the worst weather of all."

4. If the group agrees that you used the correct form of the adjective, give yourself one point and put the card at the bottom of the stack.

5. At the end of ten minutes, the player with the most points wins.

Make a Spinner

1. Put a paper clip at the center of the circle

2. Put the point of a pencil through the opening of the paper clip and at the center of the circle.

3. Hold the pencil in place and spin the paper clip to choose an adjective.

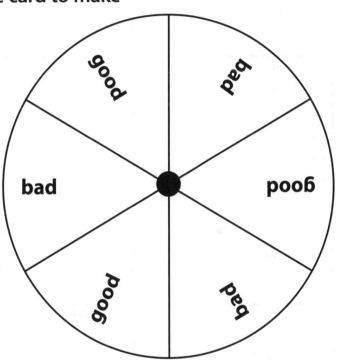

Talk about one thing.	Compare three or more things.	Compare two things.
Compare three or more things.	Compare two things.	Talk about one thing.
Compare two things.	Talk about one thing.	Compare three or more things.

Comparison Chart

Compare Media

Compare an e-mail and a Web-based news article.

	Rudy's E-Mail	"Saved in Ice"
electronic form of communication	yes	yes
formal language		
informal language		
personal information		
factual information		

 Talk with a partner. Explain whether or not you liked the article and give reasons why or why not.

Name _____ Date _____

The Storm

Grammar Rules Adjectives and Articles

Some adjectives tell "which one."

This day is warm. Was it warm **that** day?

These clouds are big. Were **those** clouds bigger?

Articles identify nouns.

An animal died in Russia.

The mammoth was about as big as **a** dog.

Write an adjective or an article in each blank.

_____ storm is starting today. _____ storm reminds me of one last year. In _____ storm, _____ inch of rain fell every hour. Then _____ rain turned into snow. Winds knocked down _____ tree, too. I hope today's storm is smaller. I hope _____ winds are softer. I like _____ tree I can see here. I want to climb _____ tree after the storm.

 Tell a partner a weather story. Include at least three adjectives and three articles.

For use with TE p. T306a

Unit 5 | Mysteries of Matter

Name _____ Date _____

http://www.ngreach.com

The Venezuelan Tar Pits Research Group

Bones from the Tar | Working at the Site | Working in the Lab | Ancient South America | **Search**

Bones from the Tar

- **Why Do Fossil Hunters Come Here?**

- **Why So Many Fossils?**

- **An Important Find**

Bones from the Tar

Why Do Fossil Hunters Come Here?

The tar pits of Venezuela, a country in South America, are a tough place to work for fossil hunters. The heat is often extreme, sometimes reaching 120°F. Why are scientists so eager to work here? The tar pits preserve fossils of a rich variety of Ice Age animals, including horses, llamas, tapirs, and other huge animals.

▲ A man is careful not to step in the naturally sticky tar.

Why So Many Fossils?

Long ago, a thick, oily material called tar seeped upward from deep underground. When the tar reached the surface, it formed pools. Rainwater collected on top of the pools, attracting animals. But when the animals tried to drink, they became trapped in the sticky tar. Ice Age meat-eaters like the scimitar cat were drawn to the struggling animals. When the meat-eaters attacked, they too became trapped in the tar. Soaked in tar, the animals' bones were preserved.

An Important Find

When Dr. Ascanio Rincon and his team recently found the bones of scimitar cats in the tar pits, they were very excited. No fossils of this animal had been found in South America before. Finding these fossils helped scientists understand how plants and animals traveled between North America and South America during the Ice Age.

Name _____ Date _____

Lisa Rubio's Field Notes

| **Home** | About Me | Pictures | Video | Contact |

March 8

CATEGORY: Tar Pits

I know I say this a lot, but I have the best job! As a member of a team of <u>tar pit</u> researchers in Venezuela, I get to discover amazing things. Don't get me wrong, it's not an easy place to work. The heat from the tar can be uncomfortable. The ground isn't even solid in many spots! Bubbles form and pop in the black ooze. It sticks to our skin, clothes, and equipment. But that nasty muck has done a great job. It's preserved the bones of creatures that lived 25,000 years ago!

3 COMMENTS   SHARE

March 12

CATEGORY: Recent Discoveries

This month the team has already made some really exciting finds! Under the leadership of Dr. Ascanio Rincon, we have found six jawbones and the skull of a <u>scimitar cat</u>. The tar has preserved the <u>fossils</u> well, but they are still fragile. So we will cover them in coats of plaster that will harden and protect them on their trip to the lab. When the fossils get there, scientists will carefully remove the plaster to study them. I'm sure they'll be as thrilled as we are to see these incredible gifts from the past.

▲ the skull of a scimitar cat

8 COMMENTS   SHARE

Search All Posts

GO

BLOG ARCHIVE

May
April
March
February
January

POSTS BY CATEGORY

Fossils
Recent Discoveries
Tar Pits

Grammar: Grammar and Writing

Edit and Proofread

Choose the Editing and Proofreading Marks you need to correct the passage. Look for correct usage of the following:

- comparison adjectives
- demonstrative adjectives
- articles

Editing and Proofreading Marks

∧	Add.
✐	Take out.
≡	Capitalize.
⊙	Add period.
∧̣	Add comma.

                    an
Lyuba is ~~a~~ amazing discovery! It is more amazinger that she
            ∧

lay quietly for thousands of years *without* being discovered. How did

she stay hidden?

Lyuba is an baby mammoth. She was found in dampest snow in

northern Russia. This region is near one of the colder regions in the

world. On this day, the temperatures there might have been warmer

than usual, causing the snow to melt.

Lyuba was only a month older when she died. Now she is

thousands of years old! It is sad that she died young, but it would

be worser if she had never been discovered. She is in the goodest

condition of any mammoth found. A scientists are happy to have

baby Lyuba.

Name _____ Date _____

Pond Ice

Grammar Rules Adjectives and Articles

• Some adjectives have special forms.	good → better than → the best bad ⟶ worse than → the worst
• To compare two things, use **-er, than,** or **more than**.	colder than more dependable than
• For adjectives that compare three or more things, use **the –est** or **the most**.	the greatest the most interesting
• Use **this** or **that** to tell "which one." Use **this** for near objects and **that** for farther objects.	this activity that book
• Use **articles** to identify a noun.	a skater the pond

Circle the correct form of the adjective or article.

1. The park here in Greenville is (better than | the best) the park ten miles south.

2. (This | That) park is smaller and doesn't have an ice rink.

3. Greenville's park has (a | an) small pond that freezes in winter.

4. Let's go into the park through (that | this) entrance right here.

5. It has (a gooder | the best) ice fishing contest for kids.

6. (A | The) pond freezes and skaters put on (an | a) ice show.

 Tell a partner about a fun place. Compare it to another place. Use a form of *good* or *bad* and *this* or *that*.

Name _____ Date _____

Why Did It Happen?

Make a cause-and-effect chart about something that happened.

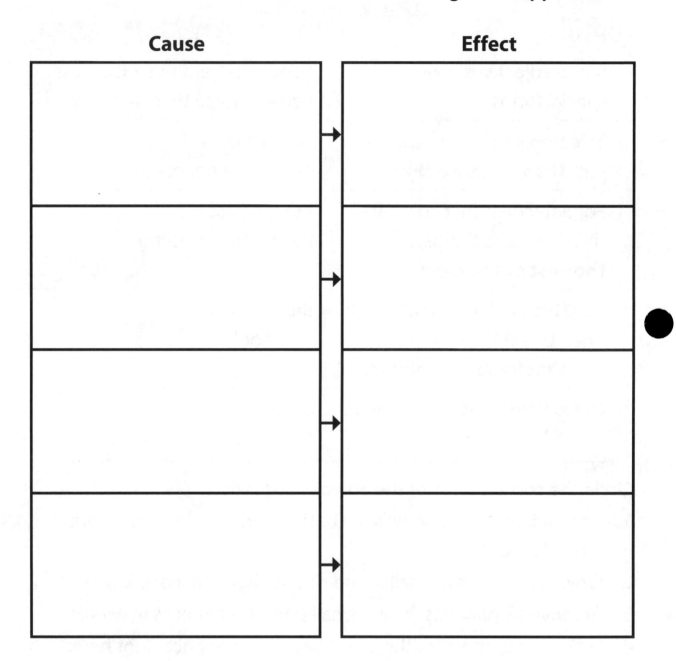

Cause   **Effect**

 Talk with a partner about a game. Tell what happened to cause another event to happen.

Name _____   Date _____

The Game Begins with a Spin

Directions:

1. Take turns. Spin for an article.

2. On your turn, choose a noun and use the article and noun in a sentence.

3. If your partner agrees that your sentence is correct, put your initials in the noun box.

Make a Spinner
1. Put a paper clip over the center of the circle.
2. Put a pencil point through a loop of the paper clip.
3. Hold the pencil firmly with one hand. Spin the paper clip with the other hand.

4. If all words that can be used for an article have been initialed, choose one to use again. Put your initials in the box too.

5. After five turns each, see who has more initialed noun boxes. Then work with your partner to see how many of the initialed nouns you can use in a story.

mixture	cloud
quicksand	marsh
substances	egg
pebbles	horse
wetland	igloos
ice cube	honor
insect	waves

Articles

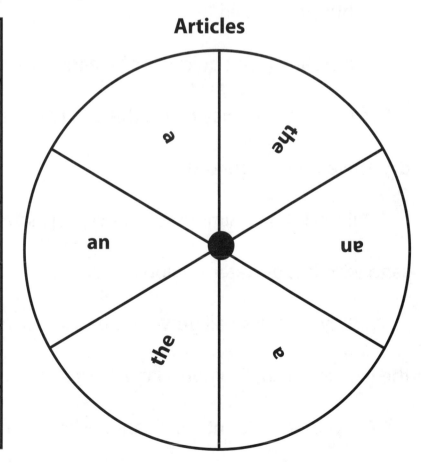

Grammar: Grammar and Writing

Edit and Proofread

Choose the Editing and Proofreading Marks you need to correct the passage. Look for correct usage of the following:

- demonstrative adjectives
- articles

Editing and Proofreading Marks

∧	Add.
℘	Take out.
≡	Capitalize.
⊙	Add period.
⋏	Add comma.

                                    the
The reporter points to a̶ sand at his feet and says, "These sand is
                          ∧

damp but pretty solid."

"Damp sand is not quicksand," a eager scientist says. She adds,

"These children are playing on this dry, hard-packed sand. If sand is

dry, there is no quicksand.

"Quicksand is an simple substance," the scientist continues. "It is

sand with lots of water around a particles."

As they enter a small grove of trees, she says, "Beyond those trees,

the land is marshy." Minutes later, their shoes are off and jeans rolled

up. A reporter walks into wet sand. "Wow! That quicksand is the

strangest thing I've ever felt."

Name _____ Date _____

Reread

Directions: Read each question about "Quicksand: When Earth Turns to Liquid." Choose the best answer.

Sample

> **1** What causes quicksand to form?
>
> Ⓐ A lot of dry sand collects in the desert.
>
> ● Underground water pushes into sand.
>
> Ⓒ Rain combines with firm sand.
>
> Ⓓ A deep area of sand reaches the surface.

2 Where is quicksand found?

Ⓐ usually at the beach   Ⓒ usually in wetlands

Ⓑ usually in a desert   Ⓓ usually in gravel

3 What happens to solid ground when quicksand starts to form?

Ⓐ It shakes.   Ⓒ It sucks you down.

Ⓑ It forms a hole.   Ⓓ It acts like a liquid.

4 Why won't you sink in quicksand?

Ⓐ Quicksand is alive.

Ⓑ Quicksand is full of bubbles.

Ⓒ The gravel will hold you up.

Ⓓ Quicksand is thicker than water.

 How did you use the test-taking strategy to answer the question?

Name _____ Date _____

"Quicksand: When Earth Turns to Liquid"

Cause	Effect
Water sinks into the sand.	

 Use your cause-and-effect chart to summarize the selection for a partner.

Name _____ Date _____

"Quicksand: When Earth Turns to Liquid"

Use this passage to practice reading with proper intonation.

The word *quicksand* makes some people shiver with fear.	9
This is probably because of the way many movies show	19
quicksand. In films, quicksand is often a mysterious substance	28
that sucks people and animals to their deaths!	36
Actual quicksand is very different from movie quicksand.	44
It rarely harms people or animals. Real quicksand is not	54
mysterious. It is a simple substance that forms naturally.	63

**From "Quicksand: When Earth Turns to Liquid,"
pages 316–317**

Fluency: Intonation

[1] ☐ Does not change pitch.　　　　[3] ☐ Changes pitch to match some of the content.

[2] ☐ Changes pitch, but does not match content.　　[4] ☐ Changes pitch to match all of the content.

Accuracy and Rate Formula
Use the formula to measure a reader's accuracy and rate while reading aloud.

$$\underline{\hspace{3cm}} - \underline{\hspace{3cm}} = \underline{\hspace{3cm}}$$

words attempted　　　　number of errors　　　　words correct per minute
in one minute　　　　　　　　　　　　　　　　　　(wcpm)

Name _____ Date _____

Play Ball!

Grammar Rules Adjectives and Articles

Some **adjectives** tell "which one" or "which ones."		near	far
	singular	**this** team	**that** team
	plural	**these** shirts	**those** shirts
Articles are words that signal nouns. • Use **the** before a noun that represents a specific thing. • Use **a** or **an** before a noun that is not specific.	**The** game starts in ten minutes. We hope to be **the** winners We can't start until **a** referee comes. She'll play **an** inning of the game. The game may be over in **an** hour.		

Read each sentence. Circle the correct form of the adjective or article.

1. (Those | These) mountains over there are solid states of matter.

2. Water is (a | an) liquid, but can become (a | an) ice cube, or a solid.

3. There are molecules in (those | this) glass of water on my desk.

4. (A | An) gas is also a state of matter.

5. What state of matter is in (that | this) balloon high up in the sky?

6. What liquids are in (these | those) containers?

7. There is (a | an) ice cream sandwich in (that | this) bag over there.

With a partner, compare an ice cube in your hand to an iceberg in a polar region. Use the adjectives <u>this</u> and <u>that</u>.

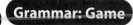

Whose Is It?

Directions:

1. Copy the words below, cut them into cards, and spread them out face up. Take turns choosing a noun (a white card) and matching a gray card to make the noun possessive.

2. Spell the possessive noun aloud. If the other players agree with your spelling, make up a phrase that includes the possessive noun and keep the white card.

   Example: *e-g-r-e-t- apostrophe -s*

   an egret's white feathers

3. If the other players don't agree, place the white card back with the other nouns.

4. Play until all white cards are gone. The winner is the one with the most cards at the end of the game.

's	'	egret	wetlands
plants	soil	families	area
birds	rocks	ocean	women
animal	surface	state	fields
parks	Jess	children	ground

Grammar: Game

Your Game? My Game? Our Game!

Directions:

1. Take turns spinning for a possessive adjective.

2. Tell if the word stands for one owner or more than one owner. Then use the word in a phrase or a sentence.

3. If other players agree that you identified the possessive adjective correctly, score one point. If they agree that you used it correctly, score another point.

4. The winner is the player with the most points at the end of the game.

Make a Spinner

1. Put a paper clip over the center of the circle.
2. Put a pencil point through a loop of the paper clip.
3. Hold the pencil firmly with one hand. Spin the paper clip with the other hand.

Possessive Adjectives

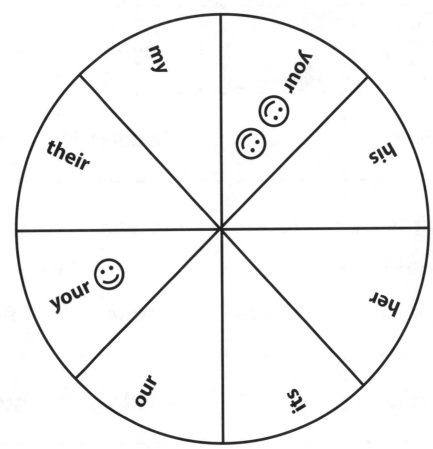

Name _____ Date _____

Compare Text Features

Compare a science article and an interview.

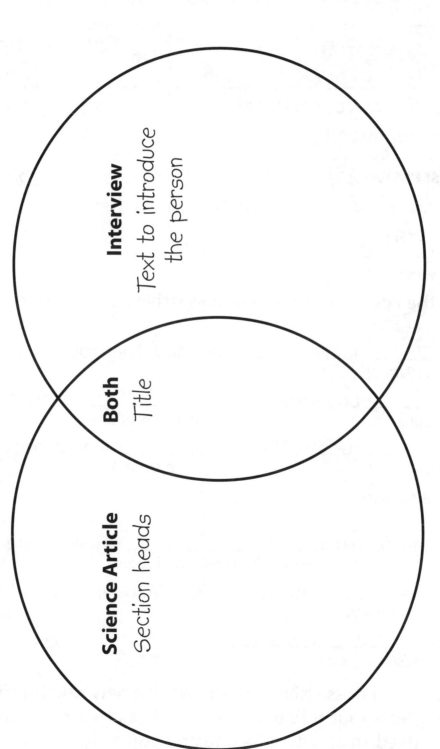

Interview

Text to introduce the person

Both

Title

Science Article

Section heads

Take turns with a partner. Interview each other about the science article and the interview. What text features did you like? Why?

Grammar: Practice

Creatures of the Wetlands

Grammar Rules Possessive Nouns and Adjectives

	One Owner	More Than One Owner
Possessive Nouns: Use an apostrophe and an *s*.	an alligator's teeth	the crabs' claws
Possessive Adjectives: Use the correct word for one or more owners.	my, your, his, her, its	our, your, their

Write the correct form of the possessive noun or adjective.

_____ family visited a wetland. They rode in two
(Nita's/Nitas')

_____ boats. Her two _____ hands tickled the
(guide's/guides')   (brother's/brothers')

_____ surface. They pulled _____ hands back when they
(water's/waters')   (his/their)

heard a splash.

    The guide said a _____ favorite tree is the
                      (mudskipper's/mudskippers')

mangrove. _____ fish story is true! Mudskippers are fish that climb
           (Her/Our)

_____ branches.
(mangrove's/mangroves')

> Use a possessive noun to write a new title for the story.
> Read your title to a partner. Check to see if your partner
> used an apostrophe and an *s* correctly.

Mark-Up Reading

Good Fences by Lisa Schneider

Biting winds. Freezing temperatures. Snowdrifts the size of houses. For people who live in Wyoming, winter can be a challenge. For animals kept outdoors there, winter can be a matter of life or death.

▲ Snow fences trap blowing snow.

Ask a Question

Eleven-year-old Erica David understood this danger because she raised goats, sheep, and pigs. Erica wanted to give her animals the best possible protection. She knew that snow fences helped to protect animals. So she wondered if snow fences could be built to work better.

Do Research

First, Erica gathered information. She learned that snow fences slow and "catch" blowing snow. This prevents snow from building up on highways or animal pens. Was there a way to catch more snow?

Form a Hypothesis

Erica thought about two possible ideas, or hypotheses, to improve snow fences. Her first idea was to change the thickness of the boards used in the fences. The second idea was to change the spacing between the boards. Next, she would test her ideas to see if either one worked.

Explanation: _____

_____

_____

_____

Mark-Up Reading
Good Fences (continued)

Test a Hypothesis

Erica built models of six fence designs. She used a fan to blow detergent "snow" onto the models. In three models, the boards were a different thickness but had the same spacing. In the other three, the thickness was the same, but the spacing between them was different. Erica observed that thick boards seemed to catch the most "snow."

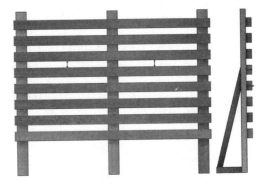

▲ Erica changed the boards' thickness and spacing.

Erica's next step was to test this idea on real snow and fences. With her dad's help, she built three, 3-foot tall snow fences. The boards were a different thickness in each fence but all had the same spacing. Erica measured the wind speeds behind each fence. The fence with the thickest boards slowed the wind the most. As a result, it caught the most snow.

Draw a Conclusion

Erica concluded that snow fences with thick boards would work best to protect her animals. Over the next several years, Erica worked to improve her snow fence designs. She even worked with a local company to see how snow fences might be used to conserve water. Today, both animals and people are benefitting from Erica's work.

Explain how ideas are related. _____

_____

_____

_____

Grammar: Grammar and Writing

Edit and Proofread

Choose the Editing and Proofreading Marks you need to correct the passage. Look for correct usage of the following:

- possessive nouns
- possessive adjectives

Editing and Proofreading Marks

∧	Add.
ℒ	Take out.
≡	Capitalize.
⊙	Add period.
⋏	Add comma.

Our teacher wanted us to see the ~~wetlands~~ wetlands' plants and animals.

She took us to her friend Shellys tour company. Shelly owns a lot of

boats, and their boats are made just for touring wetlands.

We had three guides and three boats. All of the boats rails were

high, but we could still see through them. Jose, the guide in my

boat, told us your job was really great. He said he especially liked

watching the childrens faces as they saw all of the amazing sights.

At that moment, I gasped loudly, grabbed Kriss camera, and

quickly snapped a picture. Then I showed her the picture. "It's a

photo of two alligator's tails," she exclaimed.

"It's good thing his tails were going the other way!" our guide

laughed.

Name _____ Date _____

Grammar: Reteach
Team Effort

Grammar Rules Possessive Nouns and Adjectives

• A **possessive noun** is the name of an owner.	
• For one owner, add **'s**.	a **project's** research
• For more than one owner, just add an apostrophe (**'**).	the **students'** report
• Add **'s** to some special forms of plural nouns that do not end in **s**.	**children's** notes
• A **possessive adjective** can replace an owner's name.	**one owner:** my, your, his, her, its
• Choose the possessive adjective that matches the number of owners.	**more than one owner:** our, your, their

Read each sentence. Circle the correct form.

1. We got ready to present (our | its) science project on wetlands.

2. The student had notes from (Dr. Costa's | Dr. Costas') interview.

3. "Luana, what was (you're | your) responsibility?" asked Reggie.

4. They helped Jim gather (his's | his) plant samples from the wetland.

5. "Look at this bottle," complained Maya. "(Its | It's) label is coming off."

 With a partner, discuss what makes good teamwork. Use a possessive noun and two possessive adjectives.

Name _____ Date _____

From Past to Present

Make a concept map with the answers to the Big Question:
How can we preserve our traditions?

How can we preserve our traditions?

Details Web

At a Celebration

Make a details web about things at a celebration.

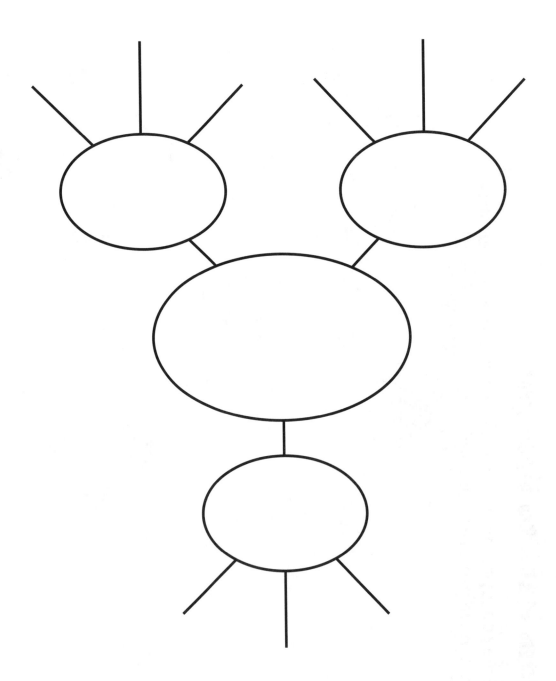

Name _____   Date _____

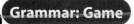

Be a Pro with Pronouns

Directions:

1. Flip a coin. For heads, move 2 squares. For tails, move 1 square.

2. Make up two sentences.

   a. The first sentence must have at least one noun.

   b. In the second sentence, replace a noun in the first sentence with the pronoun in the game square. It must agree with the noun in number and gender.

   Example: **Ricki** is a talented singer.
   He sings in the school chorus.

3. Say both sentences. If your partner agrees the pronoun is used correctly, stay in your new square. If not, return to where you were.

4. The player who reaches the end first wins.

you (one)	her	him	it
me			we
it			you (more than one)
she			they
he			us
you (one)			you (more than one)
START I			**END** them

Grammar: Grammar and Writing

Edit and Proofread

Choose the Editing and Proofreading Marks you need to correct the passage. Look for correct usage of the following:

- pronouns
- noun and pronoun agreement

Editing and Proofreading Marks

∧	Add.
℘	Take out.
≡	Capitalize.
⊙	Add period.
∧	Add comma.

In Mexican cooking, *salsa* is a sauce for foods. ~~They~~ It is a blend of ingredients with tomato as the main ingredient.

Just like in cooking, salsa music is also a blend of ingredients. In other words, they has a blend of music styles. We can have a touch of jazz, rock, and soul. But he always has a Cuban rhythm.

Most of the popular salsa singers have been male. He have many fans. The first female salsa singer to become a superstar was Celia Cruz. Cruz had a powerful voice and an exciting style of performing. These were good talents to have, and it helped her become famous. They had fans from around the world. The fans enjoyed her style of singing, and it loved her. Cruz was so popular that he became the Queen of Salsa.

Name _____ Date _____

Predict the Answer

Read the passage. As you read each question, predict the answer **BEFORE** you read the choices. Then check your prediction.

Sample

> ### The Queen of Salsa
>
> Celia Cruz was so popular that she became the "Queen of Salsa." She is my favorite singer. Celia's music reminds me of Cuba. It makes me feel happy, sad, and excited. What I like best about Celia's music is that it makes me feel like dancing!
>
> **1** What does the writer like best about Celia Cruz's music?
>
> Ⓐ It is Cuban.
>
> Ⓑ It has great rhythm.
>
> Ⓒ It makes her feel sad.
>
> ● It makes her want to dance.

2 Celia Cruz was so popular that she became _____ .

  Ⓐ known for her dancing.

  Ⓑ the "Queen of Cuban Music."

  Ⓒ my favorite singer.

  Ⓓ known as the "Queen of Salsa."

3 What does Celia's music remind the writer of?

  Ⓐ Cuba   Ⓒ being popular

  Ⓑ dancing   Ⓓ rhythm

 **How did you use the test-taking strategy to answer the question?**

Details Web

"Oye, Celia!"

Make a details web about Celia Cruz's music.

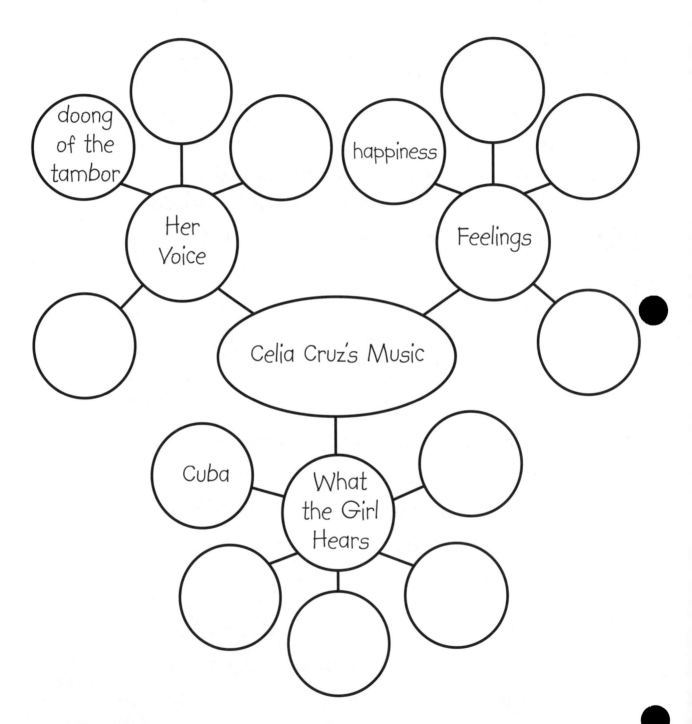

 Use your details web to describe your favorite parts of the song to a partner.

Fluency Practice

"Oye, Celia!"

Use this passage to practice reading with proper expression.

Unforgettable Celia,	2
When I hear you, I hear *la historia*—	10
Your history, my history,	14
Our history.	16
Your lyrics breathe life into our ancestors—	23
Slaves who gathered in stolen moments	29
To create a rhythm	33
That was passed down to us.	39
I thank them.	42

From "Oye, Celia!" page 358

Expression:

1 ☐ Does not read with feeling.

2 ☐ Reads with some feeling, but does not match content.

3 ☐ Reads with appropriate feeling with most content.

4 ☐ Reads with appropriate feeling for all content.

Accuracy and Rate Formula
Use the formula to measure a reader's accuracy and rate while reading aloud.

_____	−	_____	=	_____
words attempted in one minute		number of errors		words correct per minute (wcpm)

Name _____ Date _____

Dancing All Night

Grammar Rules Pronoun-Antecedent Agreement

A **pronoun** is used in place of, or to refer to, a <u>noun</u>.

Use these pronouns **for one**:	I saw an amazing <u>dance</u>!
I you she he it me you her him it	**She** saw **it** too. **It** interested **her**.
Use these pronouns **for more than one**: we you they us you them	<u>Animals</u> danced all night. **They** were in fancy clothes. The dance was fun for **them**.

Read each sentence. Write the pronoun that refers to the underlined noun.

1. <u>Animals</u> gathered in the moonlight. _____ formed a circle.

2. <u>Mr. Coyote</u> turned to Ms Fox. _____ asked her to dance.

3. <u>Ms. Fox</u> blushed a rosy red, but _____ nodded yes.

4. <u>Birds</u> of all sizes sang. We listened to _____ all night.

5. <u>Maria and I</u> grew tired, but the dance entertained _____ .

6. The <u>dance</u> was exciting. _____ had many kinds of animals.

7. <u>Maria</u> said the memory would always be with _____ .

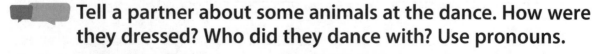 **Tell a partner about some animals at the dance. How were they dressed? Who did they dance with? Use pronouns.**

Grammar: Game

Name the Subject

Directions:

1. Copy each word below on a separate card. Mix the cards and stack them face down. Take turns picking a card.

2. Read aloud the subject pronoun and use it in a sentence. Example: "They love pizza." Then have your partner replace the pronoun in your sentence with a proper noun. Example: "Ana and Jo love pizza."

3. If you agree that your partner replaced the pronoun correctly, he or she keeps the card. If your partner did not replace the pronoun correctly, work together to correct the sentence and return the card to the bottom of the stack.

4. Play until all the cards are used. After all cards are taken, the player with more cards wins. If time allows, play another round.

I	we	you (one)
you (two or more)		she
he	it	they

Grammar: Game

A Class Act

Directions:

1. Partner 1 begins with the square numbered 1.

2. Partner 1 reads the sentence, chooses an object pronoun from the center square to fit the blank, and reads the sentence aloud.

3. If Partner 2 agrees that the sentence is correct, Partner 1 writes the pronoun on the blank line, and writes his or her initials in the square.

4. If the sentence is not correct, partners work together to choose the correct pronoun and write it on the line. Both partners write their initials in the square.

5. Next, it is Partner 2's turn, beginning with the square numbered 2, and so on. See who has more initials at the end of the game. If you have time, choose two sentences and rewrite them using different pronouns.

1. Trina, practice this solo part. It is just for _____ .	**2.** Mikey likes this song! He will learn _____ .	**3.** Olivia and I sing together. You can join _____ .
8. Class, your show is great! I am proud of _____ .	**Object Pronouns:** me you her him it us you them	**4.** Ava plays the violin. Be sure to tell _____ about the show.
7. I am making posters. I need you to help _____ .	**6.** Mia sang a new song. Then we sang with _____ .	**5.** Ask Sean and Mac to perform. We need _____ .

Name _____   Date _____

Compare Language

Compare the language used in the lyrics to the language in the biography.

Sensory Language in the Lyrics	Facts in the Biography
1. Her voice is like the doong-doong-doong of the tambor.	1. Jefferson was born in Texas.
2.	2.
3.	3.
4.	4.

 Talk with a partner about the kind of language you hear in a favorite song. Then compare that language with the language in the biography.

Grammar: Practice

My Musical Family

Grammar Rules Pronoun Agreement

	One	**More Than One**
Use **subject** pronouns in the subject of a sentence.	I, you, he, she, it	we, you, they
Use **object** pronouns in the predicate of a sentence.	me, you, him, her, it	us, you, them

What pronouns can take the place of the underlined nouns? Write the correct subject or object pronoun on the line.

1. My brother and I like music. <u>My brother and I</u> play instruments. _____

2. I play the trumpet. I have played <u>the trumpet</u> since I was six years old. _____

3. My sister plays the guitar. <u>My sister</u> strums it and sings. _____

4. My father plays the piano. Many people ask <u>my father</u> for lessons. _____

5. My grandmother is a good singer. People often invite <u>my grandmother</u> to sing. _____

 Tell a partner about people in your family and the music they like. Use subject and object pronouns correctly.

Mark-Up Reading

Moraíto Chico by Alex Hancock

Moraíto Chico was born in the town of Jerez in southern Spain in 1956. Chico became one of the greatest flamenco guitarists of his time. Flamenco music was in his blood. Both his father, Juan, and his uncle, Manuel, were well-known flamenco guitarists. He began performing when he was only 11 years old. His first performance was at a flamenco festival in Jerez. It is held every year in the dusty, open-air bullring.

▲ Moraíto Chico

Chico always stayed close to his flamenco roots in southern Spain. The region has a long tradition of flamenco music. It was brought there by people who migrated from India long ago. They carried with them their songs and dances. They also brought musical instruments such as tambourines and castenets. These instruments, with their sharp, rhythmic sounds, became part of flamenco music.

During his 40-year career, Chico played for many flamenco singers. He also performed alone. He played at flamenco festivals and recorded albums. The music he created was simple and moving. He died in 2011 after a long illness. His son Diego, also a talented flamenco guitarist, is carrying on the family tradition.

Explanation: _____

_____

_____

_____

_____

Name _____ Date _____

What I'm Listening to Now

| Home | About Me | Pictures | Video | Contact |

January 6   POSTED BY Linda Bush

▲ Castanets add their unique sound to flamenco music.

Fed up with listening to the same old tunes? Want to hear something sad and energetic at the same time? Then you should listen to a performance by Moraíto Chico. Who? This great flamenco guitarist from Spain who died last August. I just started listening, and his music is a breath of fresh air. I love those thumping, clapping, drumming sounds. If you check him out, I bet you'll become a big fan too. For real!

Just watch this online video of Chico performing on stage. You'll see sharp features framed by long, thick hair. His warm smile seems to signal a zest for life. You'll hear playing that sounds powerful but gentle. An awesome performance! Still, Chico does not try to steal the spotlight from the singers or dancers he accompanies.

You've never heard flamenco music before? Here's what it is in a nutshell. A flamenco performance mixes singing, guitars, and dancing. The guitarist strums to create flamenco's pounding rhythm. It's wild to watch flamenco dancers step, clap, and twirl to the beat. You'll get a kick out of watching Moraíto Chico play.

3 COMMENTS   SHARE

Explanation: _____

_____

_____

Name _____ Date _____

Edit and Proofread

Choose the Editing and Proofreading Marks you need to correct the passage. Look for correct usage of the following:

- subject pronouns
- object pronouns

Editing and Proofreading Marks

∧	Add.
℘	Take out.
≡	Capitalize.
⊙	Add period.
∧‚	Add comma.

I℘
You and me∧ have read about two amazing performers. Blind

Lemon Jefferson was born over one hundred years ago. Celia Cruz

was born just before Jefferson died. Her was born in Cuba. Him

was born in Texas. Him built his career with blues. Her built hers

with salsa.

We fans are loyal to both of they although their styles are very

different to we. Jefferson began a Texas blues style. Them was

brand new at the time. Cruz helped make the new salsa popular.

Their music lives on in recordings. If you want to hear she or he,

you can. Us are lucky we can hear talent like theirs from the past.

Have *you* heard either musician yet?

Grammar: Reteach

The Magical Door

Grammar Rules Subject and Object Pronouns

Use **subject pronouns** as the subject of a sentence.			
one	I you he, she, it		**I** have a map to a magical theater.
more than one	we you they		**We** can follow the trail.
Use **object pronouns** after a verb or words like *to, for, by, at*.			
one	me you him, her, it		The theater amazed **him**.
more than one	us you them		The adventure begins for **us**!

Read each sentence. Write the pronoun for the underlined nouns.

1. Skip said to Kendra, "_____ are in a strange, eerie place."

2. Kendra said to Skip, "This is where the map led _____ ."

3. Just then a fox yipped at the children. It stared at _____ .

4. The fox moved quickly. "We should follow _____ ," whispered Skip.

5. Suddenly, the children stopped. _____ saw a small, golden door, and opened it.

 Tell a partner what Skip and Kendra see behind the golden door. Use pronouns.

Flow Chart

Steps in a Process

Make a flow chart to show the steps of how to make something.

This is how to make a _____ .

Flow Chart

Step 1:

↓

Step 2:

↓

Step 3:

↓

Step 4:

Grammar: Game

Here Is This, There Is That

Directions:

1. Take turns. Spin for *this, that, these,* or *those.*

2. Use the pronoun you land on in a sentence. Point to or touch something and pretend it is a character or an object in a story. For example, if you land on *this*, pick up an eraser and say, "This is one of Jack's beans." If you land on *those*, point to three desks and say, "Those are the three pigs' houses." Use any story or movie you know for ideas.

3. If you use the pronoun correctly, score a point. Check with other players to see if you used the pronoun correctly.

4. The next player takes his or her turn. Play five rounds. Then see who got the most points. Play again if you have time.

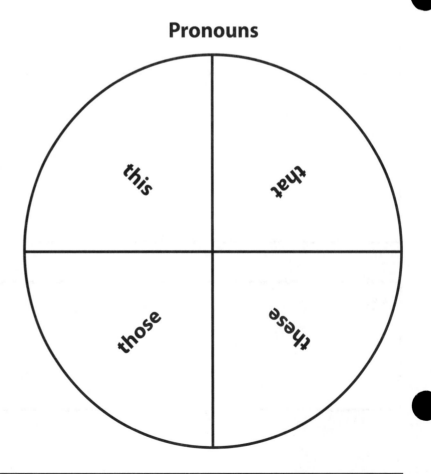

Pronouns

Make a Spinner

1. Put a paper clip over the center of the circle.
2. Put a pencil point through a loop of the paper clip.
3. Hold the pencil firmly with one hand. Spin the paper clip with the other hand.

Grammar: Grammar and Writing

Edit and Proofread

Choose the Editing and Proofreading Marks you need to correct the passage. Look for correct usage of the following:

- pronouns *this*, *that*, *these*, and *those*

Editing and Proofreading Marks

∧	Add.
℘	Take out.
≡	Capitalize.
⊙	Add period.
⋏	Add comma.

Marcy points to her book cover. "Look, Carl. ~~These~~ ^{This} is a carving."

Across the room, Carl turns from the computer. "Those is great!"

Marcy opens the book to show more photos. "This are the best

pictures of totem poles. They're all carved from cedar trunks."

"I like the colors. What shade of blue is those?" Carl asks.

"These is called teal," Marcy says pointing to the photo.

Carl points to several books beside Marcy. "What are that?"

"This tell the stories of carvings on totem poles," she says.

Carl starts across the room. "Can I borrow one of that?"

"Sure!" says Marcy, holding up a book. "I've already read that."

Name _____ Date _____

Predict the Answer

As you read each question, predict the answer **BEFORE** you read the choices. Then check your prediction by rereading "Carving Stories in Cedar."

Sample

1 What do totem pole carvers look for when they choose a tree?

Ⓐ a tree that has loose bark

Ⓑ a tree with long branches

● a tree that is tall and straight

Ⓓ a tree with red-colored leaves

2 After the totem pole is carved, what step comes next?

Ⓐ The tree is cut down.

Ⓑ The bark is removed with carving toolst.

Ⓒ Feathers are added to it.

Ⓓ It is painted.

3 Why are cranes sometimes needed to raise totem poles?

Ⓐ It is not good to touch wet paint.

Ⓑ The helpers don't have enough rope.

Ⓒ It is the traditional way.

Ⓓ Totem poles are heavy.

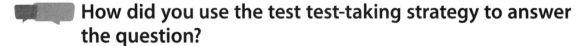 **How did you use the test test-taking strategy to answer the question?**

Flow Chart

"How to Make a Totem Pole"

Make a flow chart that tells the steps of the process.

Flow Chart

1. Shotridge chooses a design and a tree.

↓

2. He prepares the tree. He removes the bark and draws a design.

↓

[ ]

↓

[ ]

↓

[ ]

↓

[ ]

💬 **Use your flow chart to explain the steps to a partner.**

Fluency Practice

"The Legend of Raven and Fog Woman"

Use this passage to practice reading with proper intonation.

Raven asked, "How did you do that?"	7
Fog Woman didn't answer.	11
Day after day she filled the basket with water, and	21
soon the creek ran bright with salmon. No one in the	32
village went hungry.	35
But Raven wasn't satisfied. He clawed the ground with	44
his feet and flapped his wings angrily.	51
"Tell me your secret," Raven demanded.	57
Fog Woman wouldn't answer.	61
Raven lost his temper. "If you won't tell me, then go!"	72
he shouted.	74

From "The Legend of Raven and Fog Woman" pages 392–393

Intonation

1 ☐ Does not change pitch.   3 ☐ Changes pitch to match some of the content.

2 ☐ Changes pitch, but does not match content.   4 ☐ Changes pitch to match all of the content.

Accuracy and Rate Formula
Use the formula to measure a reader's accuracy and rate while reading aloud.

$$\underline{} \; - \; \underline{} \; = \; \underline{}$$

words attempted   number of errors   words correct per minute
in one minute   (wcpm)

Name _____ Date _____

Get These at This Market

Grammar Rules *this, that, these, those*

Pronouns stand alone. They can be used to point out: • a person, place, thing, or idea • more than one person, place, thing, or idea	**These** are good markers. near — far **this** — **that** **these** — **those**
Adjectives describe nouns. They can be used to tell: • which one • which ones	**These crayons** are big. near — far **this** pencil — **that** pencil **these** pens — **those** pens

Read each sentence. Circle the correct form.

1. I picked up the paintbrushes. "I want (these / those)," I told Dad.

2. "(Those / That) look nice, but we need paint first," he said.

3. "I need paint for (this / that) painting at home," I said.

4. "Yes, (that / these) is the reason for our trip," said Dad.

5. "Here is a cool easel," I said. "Can we get (those / this)?"

6. "(This / That) could be expensive," Dad sighed.

7. "But (this / these) things are for Mom's birthday," I said.

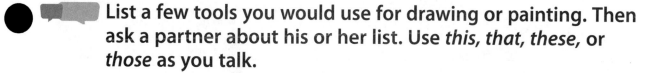 **List a few tools you would use for drawing or painting. Then ask a partner about his or her list. Use *this, that, these,* or *those* as you talk.**

Name _____ Date _____

For Anyone and Everyone

Directions:

1. Take turns flipping a coin. For heads, move 2 squares. For tails, move 1 square.

2. Use the indefinite pronoun in a sentence. Your sentence can tell about storytellers, characters, tales, or anything about stories.

3. Use a verb that matches the indefinite pronoun in number.

4. If your partner agrees that your subject and verb agree, take one more turn. If not, your partner takes his or her turn.

5. The player who reaches the end first wins.

	both	**each**	**everyone**		**any**	**END**
	anybody		**several**		**someone**	
	many		**few**		**some**	
	any		**everything**		**all**	
START	**all**		**most**	**none**	**nobody**	

Whose Turn? Yours or Mine?

Directions:

1. With a partner, copy each possessive pronoun below on a separate card.

2. Mix up the cards and place them face down in a square.

3. Take turns turning over two cards at a time and reading aloud the words. If the two words do not match, turn them face down again. Remember where they are!

4. If the two words match, use the possessive pronoun in a sentence. (Hint: Remember that a possessive pronoun stands alone, not in front of a noun.)

5. If your partner agrees that you have used the pronoun correctly, keep the cards. If not, put the cards back. The player with more cards at the end of the game wins.

mine	mine	yours	yours
his	his	hers	hers
ours	ours	its	its
yours	yours	theirs	theirs

Theme Web

Compare Themes

Compare the legend and folk tale themes.

Title: "The Legend of Raven and Fog Woman"

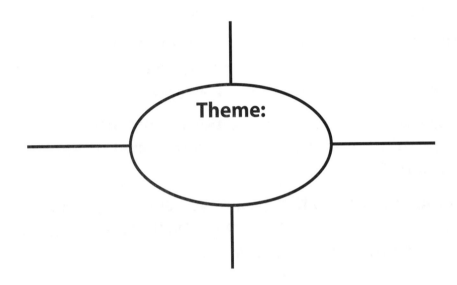

Title: "The Rainbow Bridge"

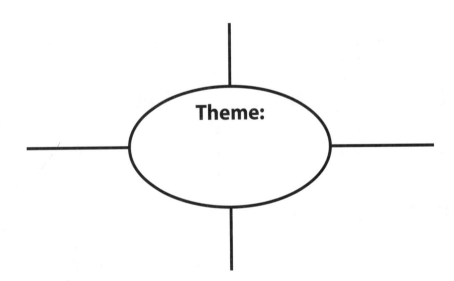

 Take turns with a partner. Use the Theme Webs to talk about how the themes of the two tales are alike and different.

Grammar: Practice

The Possessive Pronoun Game

Grammar Rules Pronoun Agreement

Use possessive pronouns to tell who or what owns something.

- For yourself, use **mine**.
- For yourself and one or more people, use **ours**.
- When you speak to one or more people, use **yours**.
- For one other person or thing, use **his**, **hers**, or **its**.
- For two or more people or things, use **theirs**.

Directions:

1. Take turns with a partner.
2. Spin the spinner.
3. Use the possessive pronoun in a sentence. If your partner agrees your wording is correct, earn 1 point.

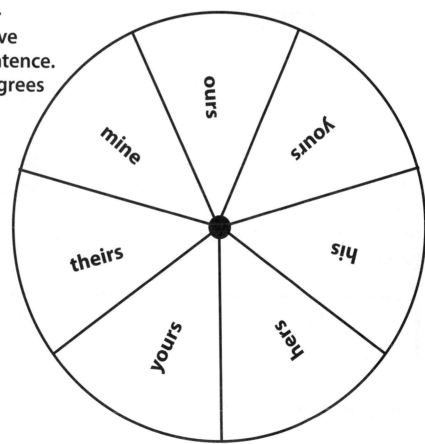

Make a Spinner

1. Put a paper clip over the center of the circle.
2. Put a pencil point through the loop of the paper clip.
3. Hold the pencil firmly with one hand. Spin the paper clip with the other hand.

Name _____   Date _____

THE FIREFLY'S LIGHT

retold by Katie Omachi

Long ago in the Philippines, there were no fireflies, and the forgetful King of the Air ruled the land.

One day, the King noticed that his ring was missing. Forgetting how forgetful he was, he suspected a thief. The King was angry. "My ring has been stolen!" he shouted. "I will reward whoever finds it."

Explanation: _____

_____

_____

The King's loyal subjects scurried away to search for the precious ring. Each wanted to be the one who won the big reward.

It was then that the King noticed a tiny fly perched on a nearby table. The sight of the trembling insect further annoyed the King. He brought his face level with the fly's.

Explanation: _____

_____

_____

THE FIREFLY'S LIGHT (continued)

"What are you doing here?" the King asked sternly. "Didn't you hear about my ring? I might order you swatted, for how could a tiny mite like you be of use to me?"

The lowly fly squeaked: "I can see with my many eyes that the ring was not stolen, my lord! Look at your crown!"

The King removed his crown, and there the ring was!

Full of gratitude, the King said, "You are the smallest of creatures, yet you saw what others did not. What reward can I offer you?"

"Oh King, I wish to stand out in some way."

The King smiled. "I will make you shine in the night, so that others will know how bright you are."

And so it was that the fly became a firefly.

Explanation: _____

_____

_____

Mark-Up Reading

THE TWO FROGS retold by Katie Omachi

Once upon a time in Japan, there were two foolish frogs. One lived in the city of Kyoto and the other in the city of Osaka. The first frog decided to travel to Osaka, and the second to Kyoto. Halfway between the cities was a steep mountain. When the travelers finally reached the top, how surprised each was to see another frog!

Explanation: _____

_____

_____

Each frog was eager to show his new friend all he knew. "No one can be certain if it's worthwhile to go on," said the Osaka frog, in a know-it-all voice. "Let's stand up and lean on each other. Then we can see where we are going."

When each frog stood and faced toward the town he wanted to visit, neither realized that his eyes now looked backwards!

Explanation: _____

_____

_____

_____

THE TWO FROGS (continued)

Soon, the frogs could hold each other up no longer. They collapsed to the ground in disappointment, not knowing that each frog had seen his own hometown.

"Dear me! Kyoto is just like Osaka!" the Osaka frog declared with certainty.

"And Osaka is just the same as Kyoto," said the Kyoto frog, wanting to have the last word.

"If I had known that, I would not have traveled all this way," said the Osaka frog, wanting to have the last word himself.

"Nor I," said the Kyoto frog. "It is truly a disappointment to have made such a long journey."

And so the frogs' conversation went on and on until each was so exhausted that he could not say another word. Then the frogs shook hands to mark their important discovery.

So each frog went home feeling even wiser because of all he had learned. They would always believe that Osaka and Kyoto—which are as different as two towns can be—were as alike as two peas.

Explanation: _____

_____

_____

_____

Grammar: Grammar and Writing

Edit and Proofread

Choose the Editing and Proofreading Marks you need to correct the passage. Look for correct usage of the following:

- indefinite pronoun
- possessive pronoun

Editing and Proofreading Marks

∧	Add.
℘	Take out.
≡	Capitalize.
⊙	Add period.
∧̣	Add comma.

"Luis and Bea have a folk-tale to tell. This version is their. All of

you listens closely," says Ms. Cole. Luis and Bea tell the story:

"Little Bear, this chair is mines!" cries Goldilocks. "It is not your.

You will crush it. Everyone know that."

"That is Papa's footstool. No one else think it's yours!" says Little

Bear. "Aren't I right, Mama Bear? This stool is not she's! Papa Bear

needs this. It's he's."

Creak! The children turn as the door opens. Papa Bear comes in.

"We have a visitor again, I see," says Papa Bear. "Few comes as often

as you, Goldilocks."

"My family's home is nice," says Goldilocks. "But our is quiet, and

your is fun." Mama and Papa Bear laugh.

Grammar: Reteach

A Storytelling Contest

Grammar Rules Indefinite and Possessive Pronouns

Use an **indefinite pronoun** when you are not naming a specific person or thing.	**Many** of the stories are great.
• Some are always <u>plural</u>. ⟶	both few many several
• Some are always <u>singular</u>. ⟶	anybody each everyone everything nobody someone
• Some can be either. ⟶	all any most none some
Use a **possessive pronoun** to replace the name of an owner and what the owner has.	<u>Lenny's story</u> is unusual. **His** is a folk tale.
• one owner ⟶	mine yours hers his its
• more than one owner ⟶	ours yours theirs

Read each sentence. Circle the correct possessive pronoun or the correct verb to agree with the indefinite pronoun.

1. Rod chooses a story to tell. "This is (mine / his)," he says proudly.

2. Len and Ming are going to tell a story together. (Theirs / There's) will be funny.

3. <u>All</u> of the stories should (take / takes) 10 minutes to tell.

4. <u>Many</u> students (plans / plan) to enter the storytelling contest.

 Tell a partner about a story you would like to tell. Use at least two indefinite pronouns and possessive pronouns.

Name _____ Date _____

Blast! Crash! Splash!

Make a concept map with the answers to the Big Question.

What forces can change Earth?

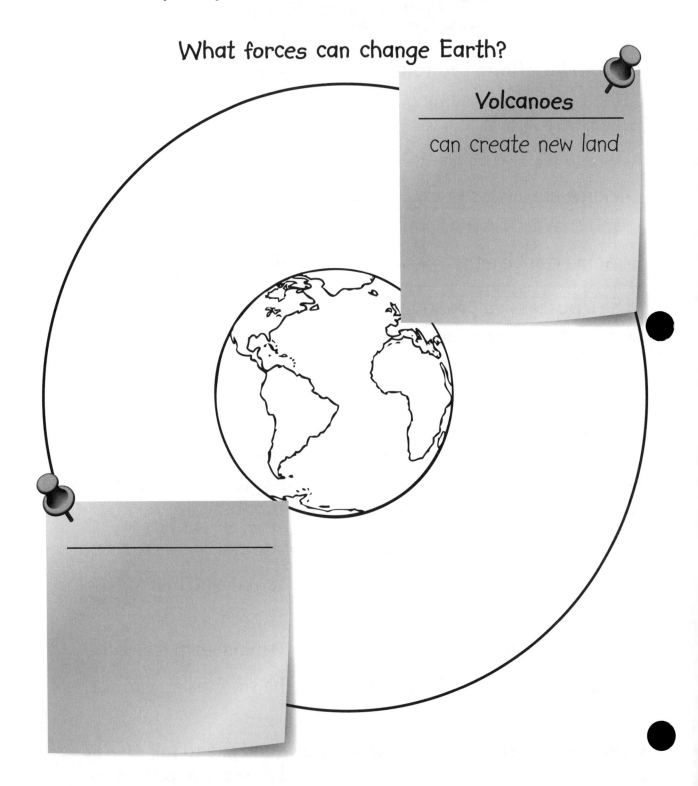

Volcanoes
_____

can create new land

_____

Imagery Chart

Title: _____

Make an imagery chart about your story.

Place	Person	Thing

 Use imagery to tell your partner another story.

Grammar: Game

Word Cards

Directions:

1. Copy the grid below on gray and white paper and cut out the cards. Place the white adverb cards facedown in a stack. Arrange the gray cards, facing up, on a desk.

2. Select a white card. Match the adverb with a gray card, then say a sentence using the adverb.

3. If your partner agrees that the match and sentence are correct, keep the white card. If not, return the card to the bottom of the stack.

4. Take turns playing until all the cards have been matched.

how	when	where
suddenly	nervously	down
everywhere	today	quickly
yesterday	around	now
roughly	up	loudly

Grammar: Grammar and Writing

Edit and Proofread

Choose the Editing and Proofreading Marks you need to correct the passage. Look for the following:

correct use of adverbs

Editing and Proofreading Marks

∧	Add.
ℐ	Take out.
⌒∧	Move to here.
⋏	Add comma.

For weeks, we sail brave across the sea. The voyage is exciting very.

Waves and wind rock our wildly ship. Rain pours down.

Now it is morning. I stand silent on the deck of the ship. The

dense fog lifts soon than it did yesterday. Then I notice something in

the distance. I shout loud, "Land!"

Our finally ship comes close to shore. The water looks cold, but

my friend and I dive in. I swim more fast than my friend so I get

to the island quickly than he does. It is a beautiful very island. Big

above birds fly. Trees and flowers gentle sway in the breeze. Soon

many more people will come. But today, the island is ours!

© National Geographic Learning, a part of Cengage Learning, Inc.

For use with TE p. T411p   **PM7.4**   **Unit 7** | Blast! Crash! Splash!

Name _____ Date _____

Read All Choices

Read the sample passage and each question. Then choose the best answer.

Sample

> At first, no one lived on the island. Then a fishing boat came. The fisherman liked the island. There were fruit trees and plants to eat. He thought, "I will bring my family here to live." Other families came. Soon a community of people lived on the island.

1 What conclusion can you draw?
  - Ⓐ The island is very small.
  - Ⓑ The man is a good fisherman.
  - ● The man's family needed a better place to live.

2 Why will the island be a good place for families to live?
  - Ⓐ There will be plenty of food.
  - Ⓑ There is a fishing boat on the island.
  - Ⓒ They will have a big house.

3 What is the main idea of the passage?
  - Ⓐ The island became a home to many families.
  - Ⓑ The families planted gardens.
  - Ⓒ There was food and celebration.

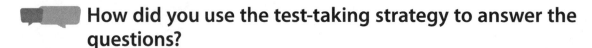 **How did you use the test-taking strategy to answer the questions?**

Imagery Chart

"An Island Grows"

Make an imagery chart of "An Island Grows."

Volcano	Land	Plants	Animals	People
Stone breaks. Water quakes.				

 Use your imagery chart to talk with a partner about your favorite parts of the poem.

Fluency: Intonation

"An Island Grows"

Use this passage to practice reading with proper intonation.

Sailors spot.	2
Maps plot.	4
Ships dock.	6
Traders flock.	8
Settlers stay.	10
Children play.	12
Workers build.	14
Soil is tilled.	17
Markets sell.	19
Merchants yell.	21
"Fresh fish!"	23
"Pepper dish!"	25
"Ripe fruit!"	27
"Spicy root!"	29

From "An Island Grows," pages 426-428

Intonation

1 ☐ Does not change pitch.

2 ☐ Changes pitch, but does not match content.

3 ☐ Changes pitch to match some of the content.

4 ☐ Changes pitch to match all of the content.

Accuracy and Rate Formula

Use the formula to measure a reader's accuracy and rate while reading aloud.

$$\frac{}{\text{words attempted in one minute}} - \frac{}{\text{number of errors}} = \frac{}{\substack{\text{words correct per minute} \\ \text{(wcpm)}}}$$

Name _____ Date _____

Grammar: Reteach

The Bicycle Race

Grammar Rules Adverbs

An **adverb** describes a verb. It can come before or after a verb and tells *how, where,* or *when.*	Miguel pedals **quickly**. Matt **sometimes** rests.
Sometimes an adverb tells more about an adjective or another adverb.	Denny pedals **very slowly**.
To compare two actions, add **-er** or use **more** or **less**.	Rosa pedals **harder** up the hills than down. Rosa practices **less often** than Miguel.

Read each sentence. Circle the correct word to complete the sentence.

1. Miguel begins the race (eagerly/eager).

2. Rosa races (easy/easily) to the lead.

3. Denny steers (more careful/very carefully) on the muddy road.

4. Rosa waits (patiently/patient) at the finish line.

5. Rosa will (happy/happily) coach the other racers for the next race.

 With a partner, discuss the bike race. Take turns using adverbs to describe the different bike riders.

Grammar: Game

Spin to Choose Adverbs

Directions:

1. Play with a partner. First, make a spinner for the game.
   - Draw a circle on a piece of heavy paper or cardboard. Divide it into 4 equal sections numbered 1 through 4.
   - Fasten a brad through the center of the circle.
   - Hook a large paper clip over the brad on the front.

2. Each player spins three times. The first spin is for a number from box A. The second spin is for B, and the third is for C.

3. The player uses the numbered choices to create a sentence that compares actions.

   Example:

   A player spins A-1, B-2, and C-4 and creates this sentence:

   The <u>mud</u> <u>fell</u> **more quickly** than the <u>ash</u>,
   but the <u>rocks</u> <u>fell</u> **most quickly** of all.

4. Continue the game until each player creates five sentences.

5. Choose two of your favorite sentences to display in the room.

A. Nouns	**B. Verbs**	**C. Adverbs**
1. ash, rocks, mud	**1.** shook	**1.** angrily
2. trees, crops, lakes	**2.** fell	**2.** swiftly
3. bridges, roads, sidewalks	**3.** pounded	**3.** quickly
4. trucks, cars, tractors	**4.** disappeared	**4.** noisily

Grammar: Game

Adverb Race

Directions:

1. Each player writes five verbs, each on a separate card. Mix up all the cards and place them facedown in a stack.

2. Use an eraser or other small object as a game piece. Flip a coin. Move one space for heads. Move two spaces for tails.

3. Draw a card. Create a sentence using the verb and the comparison adverb on the board. If the other players agree that your sentence is correct, stay on the space. If your sentence is incorrect, go back one space.

4. Take turns. The first one to reach THE END wins.

BEGIN	well	better	best	well
				better

well	best	better	well	best
better				
best	well	better	best	THE END

Name _____   Date _____

Compare Texts

Write details from each text. Add a star to details that are similar in both texts.

"An Island Grows"	"Volcano Views"
Tells about volcanoes under the sea	Tells about a man who photographs volcanoes
*Tells about magma and lava	*Tells about magma and lava

 Talk with a partner. Tell each other which text you liked better and why.

Grammar: Adverbs

Volcanoes Rock!

Grammar Rules Adverbs

Adverbs tell more about a verb.

Islands grow **slowly**. (tells how)

Some lava flows **faster** than other lava. (compares two actions)

Thick lava flows the **least quickly** of all. (compares three or more actions)

Underline the adverbs.

I am a scientist. I see volcanoes erupt. I saw one yesterday. The ground rumbled loudly. Rocks soon flew out. The lava flowed more quickly than any lava I have seen. It glowed brightly.

The lava flows more slowly today. Ash floats everywhere. It is an amazing sight!

 Write three sentences about forces of nature. Use adverbs. Read your sentences to a partner.

▲ Mount St. Helens erupts.

Life Returns to
Mount St. Helens
By Andreas Pilar

On a visit to Mount St. Helens today, you see a quiet volcano and green forest. But what if you been there on May 18, 1980? You would have heard a powerful bang as the volcano erupted. You would have seen the entire north face of the volcano collapse. You would have seen hot gas, ash, and steam moving across the landscape at 200 miles an hour. The forest would have disappeared before your eyes.

After the eruption, the area around Mount St. Helens seemed lifeless. A thick layer of gray ash covered the land. But scientists studying the destruction within weeks of the eruption quickly discovered that life had already returned.

Plants began to reappear in the summer of 1980. When the volcano erupted, snow still covered the ground. Some small trees and shrubs were protected beneath this snowpack. As the snow melted, these plants appeared. In other places, seeds carried by wind or animals began to sprout.

▲ Flowers bloom around Mount St. Helens today.

Life Returns to
Mount St. Helens

(continued)

Plants weren't the only things to survive. Many smaller animals, such as gophers and toads, survived the blast. These animals were hibernating when the volcano erupted. They awoke to find their world completely gone. Then they quietly went to work.

Gophers digging tunnels brought up fertile soil from below the ash cover. This rich soil mixed with the ash and helped new plants to grow. In 1998, park rangers reported on the recovery. They found that larger animals such as elk, deer, and bear had returned as their food supplies increased. Elk also helped to speed up plant recovery by uncovering soil and seeds with their hooves.

In May, 2005, twenty-five years after the major eruption, scientists were amazed at the recovery around Mount St. Helens. Viginia Dale, ecologist, counted more than 150 kinds of wildflowers, shrubs and trees. Today, the volcano is still quiet. But no one is fooled by the sleeping giant. Mount St. Helens could again transform the landscape with a single, mighty blast.

Today

2005

2000

1990

1980

Grammar: Grammar and Writing

Edit and Proofread

Choose the Editing and Proofreading Marks you need to correct the passage. Look for the following:

- correct use of adverbs that compare
- correct use of irregular adverbs

Editing and Proofreading Marks

∧	Add.
୭	Take out.
⊙	Add period.
∧̣	Add comma.

Last night, I watched the ~~scarier~~ scariest news report I've ever seen. The

report showed very dramatic views of a volcano erupting. One video

showed it better of all. The volcano was the larger volcano in the

entire island chain of Hawaii. Clouds of black smoke and ash floated

everywhere. Some villagers coughed loudly from smoke. Other

villagers coughed even most loudly than others. A large river of lava

flowed down one side of the volcano. A smallest river of lava flowed

down another side. But the more disturbing thing of all was the

location of the village. It was right between the two rivers of lava! I

think the lava is the scarier part of any volcano.

Grammar: Reteach

Jump High, Fox!

Grammar Rules Adverbs

An **adverb** tells **how**, **where**, or **when**.	Fox ran <u>quickly</u> <u>here</u> <u>yesterday</u>.
An **adverb** can tell **about** an **adjective**.	Fox ate a <u>very</u> <u>small</u> meal.
An **adverb** that **compares two actions** uses **–er**. An **adverb** that **compares three or more actions** uses **–est**.	Red Robin sat high<u>er</u> than Fox. Crow perched the high<u>est</u> of all.
An **adverb** that ends in **-ly** and **compares two actions**, uses **less** or **more**. An **adverb** that ends in **-ly** and **compares three or more actions**, uses **least** or **most**.	Crow ate <u>less</u> quick<u>ly</u> than Fox. Fox ate <u>more</u> quick<u>ly</u> than Crow. Fox ate <u>least</u> calm<u>ly</u> of all animals. He ate <u>most</u> eager<u>ly</u> of all.
A **few adverbs** have **special forms** for comparing.	well → better → best badly → worse → worst

Circle the word or phrase that completes each sentence.

1. Fox trotted _____ to a grapevine hanging from an arch.
   (calm/calmly)

2. The _____ red, ripe grapes hung high out of Fox's reach.
   (really/real)

3. Crow said the grapes hung _____ than foxes jump.
   (more high/higher)

4. Fox jumped the _____ of all foxes.
   (more gracefully/most gracefully)

Name _____ Date _____

Underwater Earthquakes

Make a cause-and-effect chart for the diagram on page 445. In the last row of your chart, predict one cause-and-effect relationship not shown on the chart.

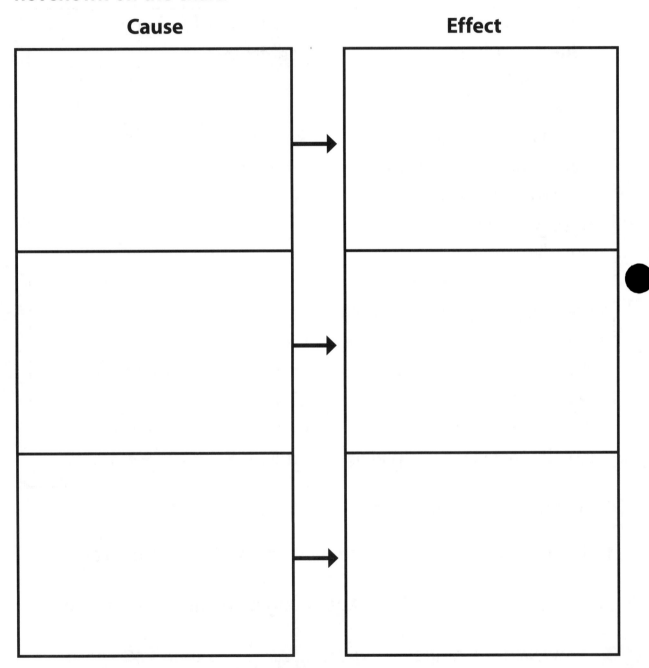

Cause	Effect

 Use your chart to tell a partner about one cause-and-effect relationship related to a tsunami.

For use with TE p. T445a   **PM7.17**   **Unit 7** | Blast! Crash! Splash!

Grammar: Game

Match and Say

Directions:

1. Copy the grid below on gray and white paper. Cut out the word cards and place them face down.

2. Taking turns, pick one gray card and one white card. Form a sentence using the adjective on the gray card, for example: *The steady sun shines*. Then, form another sentence using the adverb on the gray card, for example: *The sun shines steadily*. If you like, add details to your sentence.

3. If the group agrees that you used the words correctly, keep the card. If not, put it back in the pile.

4. Play until all the cards are taken. The player with the most cards wins.

angry | angrily	bad | badly	quick | quickly
steady | steadily	gentle | gently	easy | easily
sun shines	hawk escaped	tree fell
wind blows	brother worked	cat caught

Grammar: Grammar and Writing

Edit and Proofread

Choose the Editing and Proofreading Marks you need to correct the passage. Look for the following:

- correct use of adjectives and adverbs
- correct use of adjectives and adverbs that compare

Editing and Proofreading Marks

∧	Add.
℘	Take out.
⊙	Add period.

    Rumble! Crash! Scott started walking very slow∧^{ly} "What was that?" he asked Rose.

    "It sounded like something exploded loud," she said. Both looked at the mountains behind them. They saw a real huge cloud of black smoke far in the distance.

    "I think that volcano just erupted!" said Rose. Her eyes were the most big Scott had ever seen. Scott grabbed his sister's arm tight. "Don't worry," Rose said. "It's very far away." But Scott didn't feel very safely. He just wanted to hide quiet under a bed. Just then, their mom arrived. She looked calmly.

    "That volcano is too far away to cause us any harm," she told Scott and Rose. Scott was so happily to hear that! But he still hugged his mom the most tight he had ever hugged her.

Name _____ Date _____

Read All Choices

Read each question and choose the best answer.

Sample

1 What happens first after Dinakaran runs back to the house?

- ● Selvakumar barks and howls at Dinakaran.
- Ⓑ Dinakaran and Selvakumar run up the hill together.
- Ⓒ Selvakumar drags Dinakaran outside the house.
- Ⓓ Papa and Mama both shout "Run!" at the same time.

2 Dinakaran goes back into the house because _____

- Ⓐ Papa told him to go into the house.
- Ⓑ he doesn't hear Mama properly.
- Ⓒ he thinks it is safer in the house.
- Ⓓ Selvakumar nudged him towards the house.

3 Which sentence belongs on the blank lines of the chart below?

- Ⓐ Selvakumar barks and howls at Dinakaran.
- Ⓑ Selvakumar sensed the tsunami.
- Ⓒ An earthquake shook the ground.
- Ⓓ The village is destroyed.

Cause	Effect
A tsunami comes to the village.	_____

Name _____   Date _____

"Selvakumar Knew Better"

Make a cause-and-effect chart for "Selvakumar Knew Better."

Cause		Effect
Selvakumar hears a sound.	→	He whines and barks to warn his family.
Papa shouts, "Tsunami! Run!"	→	
	→	
	→	
	→	

 Use your chart to tell a partner about one cause and effect.

Fluency: Practice

"Selvakumar Knew Better"

Use this passage to practice reading with proper intonation.

As Dinakaran and Selvakumar rested, they heard the	8
grownups talking.	10
"We'll never recover," moaned one man.	16
"We've lost absolutely everything," someone else said.	23
But Selvakumar felt the regular rhythm of Dinakaran's	31
chest rising and falling under his chin. Then he heard	41
Dinakaran's little brothers nearby. He smelled the familiar	49
scents of Papa and Mama.	54
And Selvakumar knew better.	58

From "Selvakumar Knew Better," page 462

Intonation

[1] ☐ Does not read with feeling.

[2] ☐ Reads with some feeling, but does not match content.

[3] ☐ Reads with appropriate feeling for most content.

[4] ☐ Reads with appropriate feeling for all content.

Accuracy and Rate Formula
Use the formula to measure a reader's accuracy and rate while reading aloud.

$$\underline{\hspace{3cm}} - \underline{\hspace{3cm}} = \underline{\hspace{3cm}}$$

words attempted   number of errors   words correct per minute
in one minute   (wcpm)

Grammar: Reteach

Grammar Rules Adjectives, Adverbs

- An adjective describes a noun: *small.*
- An adjective that compares two things uses -er. If the adjective has 3 or more syllables, it uses more or less: *bigger, more colorful.*
- An adjective that compares three or more things uses -est. If it has 3 or more syllables, it uses most or least: *biggest, most forgetful.*
- A few adjectives have special forms for comparing: *good, better, best: bad, worse, worst.*
- An adverb tells how, where, or when: *very, nearby, yesterday.*
- An adverb that compares two actions uses -er. If the adverb ends in -ly, it uses more or less: *faster, less loudly.*
- An adverb that compares three or more actions uses -est. If the adverb ends in -ly, it uses most or least: *fastest, most quickly.*
- A few adverbs have special forms for comparing: *well, better, best; badly, worse, worst.*

Circle the word or phrase that completes each sentence.

1. Mia, Ana, and I spent one _____ night sleeping outside.
   (scary/scariest)

2. Crickets sang _____ than I thought they could.
   (more loudly/most loudly)

3. Ana and Mia slept _____ curled up in cozy sleeping bags.
   (good/well)

4. Suddenly, furry monsters dashed _____ by. Really!
   (swiftly/more swifter)

Grammar: Game

Everything Changes

Follow the steps below to create your own comic strip.

Step 1: Choose characters from the box below.

Mouse	Cat	Dog	Rabbit	Fox	Wolf

Step 2: Use a preposition from the box below to give at least one <u>detail</u> about the relationship of the characters.

Example: *Mouse knew <u>about</u> Cat's sharp teeth.*

for	like	of	about	from	except	besides

Step 3: Use a preposition from the box below to tell the <u>time</u> the chase starts.

Example: *<u>By</u> noon, Mouse heard Cat's claws on the sidewalk.*

during	after	until	since	by

Step 4: Use a preposition from the box below to describe the <u>direction</u> of the chase.

Example: *Mouse scurried <u>from</u> the house <u>to</u> the backyard.*

into	to	out	off	from
around	inside	outside	below	above

Step 5: Now imagine that suddenly the earth rolls and rumbles. An earthquake! Choose prepositions from the box in step 4 to describe how the chase changes.

Step 6: Draw pictures to represent each part of your story.

Grammar: Game

Show the Relationship

Direction	Where	Time	Details
to	above	at	about
through	below	before	for
by	under	after	of
toward	in	during	from

Directions:

1. Teams have ten minutes. One team answers the odd-numbered questions below. The other team answers the even-numbered questions. Use "Tsunami," on Anthology pages 467-471 to find the facts.

2. Write your answers using prepositional phrases. Use prepositions from the chart or choose others you know.

3. When time is up, underline each prepositional phrase and circle each preposition.

4. Count the phrases your team used. The team with more correct prepositional phrases wins.

Questions:

1. What is a tsunami?

2. What causes a tsunami?

3. When is energy produced underwater?

4. In what direction does the force push?

5. Where do the waves go?

6. Tell what you know about the waves.

7. What states are at greatest risk for tsunamis?

8. Where can you find two tsunami warning centers?

9. What do warning centers do?

Name _____ Date _____

Compare Texts

Compare "Selvakumar Knew Better" and "Tsunami."

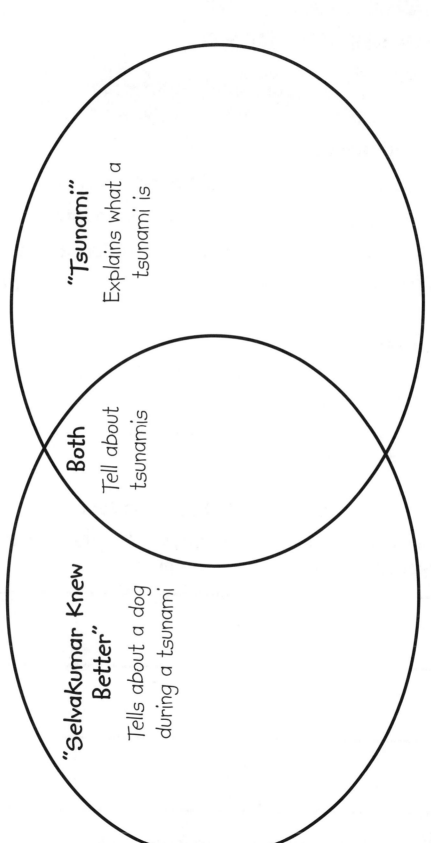

"Tsunami"
Explains what a tsunami is

Both
Tell about tsunamis

"Selvakumar Knew Better"
Tells about a dog during a tsunami

Tell a partner which text you liked better and why.

Name _____ Date _____

Preposition Bingo

Grammar Rules Prepositional Phrases

Prepositional phrases:

- tell where   ⟶   Jean's purse is **under the seat**.
- show direction   ⟶   The man walked **into the store**.
- show time   ⟶   My cat sleeps **during the day**.
- add details   ⟶   Greg added some pepper **to the stew**.

Directions:

1. Write one preposition in each box: *into, on, before, after, to, across, over, under, during.*

2. Your teacher or another student says a sentence with a prepositional phrase. Listen for the preposition in the sentence.

3. Put an "X" in the box with that preposition.

4. Once you have a complete row, yell "Bingo!" and use each preposition in the row in a sentence.

 Point to a preposition in your chart. Have your partner use it in a sentence.

Name _____   Date _____

Ready for an Emergency?   by Liliana Klein

Have you wondered if you really need to have supplies ready in case a disaster strikes your town? Well, I can tell you that when my family was trapped by a flood last year, we would not have made it without our emergency kit. Whether it is a blackout or an earthquake, you must have an emergency kit with these basic supplies.

In an emergency, you may not have clean water available, so you must stock water and canned food items. Emergency experts recommend one gallon of water per person per day. Canned foods such as ready-to-eat vegetables are healthy and last a long time.

What if someone gets hurt? You need a first-aid kit to deal with injuries. Your first-aid kit should include bandages, a thermometer, and antibiotics.

In case you lose power, you should have a flashlight and batteries. Use a waterproof container to store your supplies, such as a sealable plastic bag. And don't forget to add warm clothes, soap, and cell phone chargers. Being prepared will save your life.

The author's purpose is _____.

◀ A disaster emergency kit should include essential supplies.

Name _____ Date _____

Preparing for a Disaster   By Roberto Samuels

Following a disaster, it is sad to hear victims say, "if only we had been better prepared." Being prepared can make the difference between life and death. One of the best ways to prepare is for every family to create an emergency communication plan. To make an emergency communication plan for your family, first discuss what kinds of disasters might threaten your area. Do destructive windstorms, such as tornadoes, often strike your community? Do you live on a coast where undersea earthquakes might cause tsunami waves? Different disasters require different responses that will affect communication needs.

Next, choose a place in your neighborhood where your family could meet in an emergency in case you become separated. You might choose a familiar shop, such as a local grocery or drugstore. Then pick an out-of town contact person. Program that contact into your cell phone. Label this person under the name "ICE." This stands for "in case of emergency." Finally, teach young children how to make phone calls and send text messages to your emergency contact and to the police. Now, you're ready for anything!

The author's purpose is _____
_____
_____

◀ Tsunami waves can be powerful enough to destroy a house.

Name _____ Date _____

Edit and Proofread

Choose the Editing and Proofreading Marks you need to correct the passage. Look for the following:

- correct use of prepositions
- correct use of prepositional phrases

Editing and Proofreading Marks

∧	Add.
ℐ	Take out.
⊙	Add period.
⋀	Add comma.

There is an odd thing about tsunamis. You can't see them if you
are with deep ocean waters. Their waves are only a few feet high. If a

ship is far from land, it can sail right from the tsunami's waves. No one

on the ship can feel it over their feet!

Tsunamis can travel on jet speed and jet speed is fast! Tsunamis

have been measured at speeds upon 500 miles per hour! The waves

of a tsunami can be very large? The 100-foot waves can reach out

the sky. Tsunamis can travel with the entire Pacific Ocean in less than

a day! This is why people need to be warned beside a tsunami ever

reaches land.

Grammar: Reteach

A Town Mural

Grammar Rules Prepositions

A **prepositional phrase** starts with a preposition and ends with a noun or a pronoun. The preposition is used to show the relationship of the noun or pronoun to another word in the sentence.

• A prepositional phrase can tell where.	→ Our art class is painting a <u>mural</u> **on** the community center <u>building</u>.
• It can show direction.	→ We <u>walk</u> **through** the <u>courtyard</u>.
• It can show time.	→ Everyone <u>paints</u> **during** our art <u>class</u>.
• It can add other details.	→ Our teacher takes <u>photographs</u> **for** the <u>newspaper</u>.

Circle the word or phrase that completes each sentence. Underline the noun in the prepositional phrase and then underline the word it tells something about.

1. We chose (among/upon) different ideas that were presented.

2. Nearly everyone voted (over/for) the undersea mural.

3. There are many colorful fish and plants (during/under) the ocean's surface.

4. The mural stretches (across/on) the whole courtyard wall.

5. We needed a good plan so we wouldn't bump (toward/ against) each other as we worked.

6. We divided (into/out) three groups.

 Tell a partner about a project you liked. Use three prepositional phrases to help you tell about it.

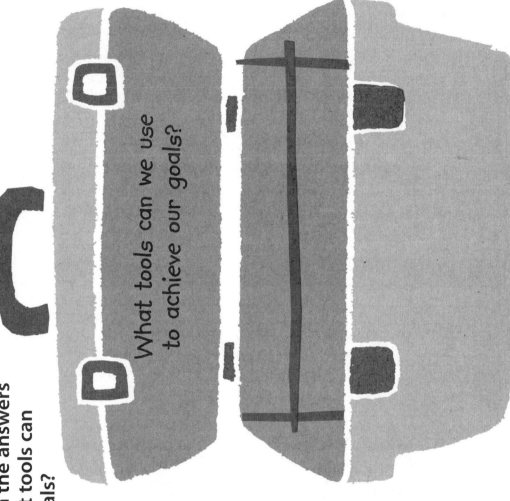

What tools can we use to achieve our goals?

Getting There

Make a concept map with the answers to the Big Question: What tools can we use to achieve our goals?

For use with TE p. T483

PM8.1

The Big Race

Make a story map about a goal and outcome in life.

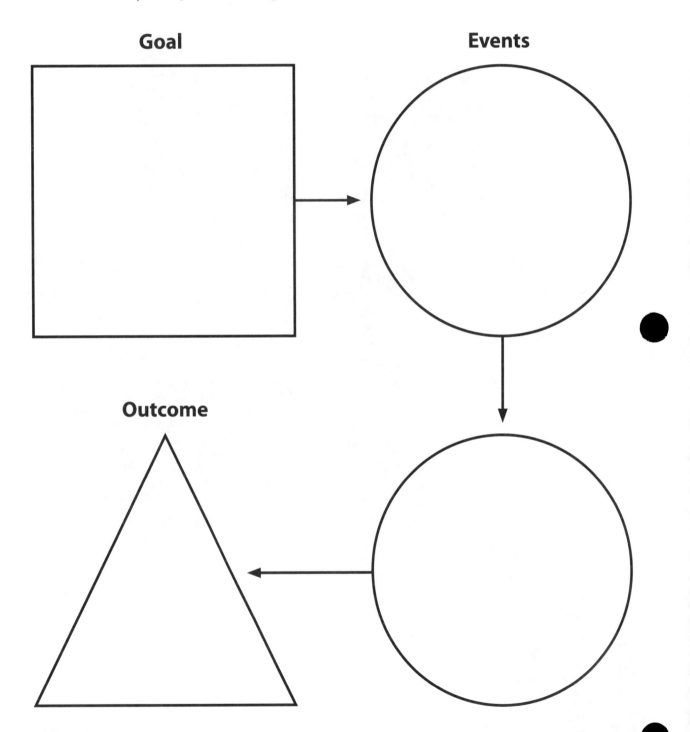

Goal

Events

Outcome

 Talk with a partner about how each event relates to the goal and the outcome.

Name _____   Date _____

You Started Here and Ended There

Directions:

1. Take turns flipping a coin. For heads, move 2 squares. For tails, move 1 square.

2. Spell the past-tense form of the verb in the square. Then use the past-tense verb in a sentence.

3. If your partner agrees the verb is spelled and used correctly, take one more turn. If not, your partner takes his or her turn.

4. The player who reaches the end first wins.

END

hurry	stay	enjoy		play
divide		subtract		stop
shrug		operate		classify
trip		multiply		obey
add		reply	beg	chase

START

Grammar: Grammar and Writing

Edit and Proofread

Choose the Editing and Proofreading Marks you need to correct the passage. Look for correct usage of the following:

- regular past-tense verbs

Editing and Proofreading Marks

∧	Add.
ℐ	Take out.
≡	Capitalize.
⊙	Add period.
⋏	Add comma.

Yesterday afternoon, Ms. Sophy ~~pass~~ passed out math problems. She

enjoy the math lesson that morning and hope the children could do

the problems. They study the problems carefully. Pencils began to

make a *scritch-scratch* sound. The children added and subtract, and

they multiply and divided.

As students finish, Ms. Sophy sent them outside. A few grab each

other's hands and ran in circles until they fell down laughing. They all

jumped up and play again. One boy organize a game of tag. Runners

zigzagged everywhere until the boy finally tag a player.

At that moment, Ms. Sophy walked out. One of the girls cry out,

"Tell us about your first day of school again, Ms. Sophy!"

Name _____   Date _____

Skip and Return to Questions

Directions: Read each question about "Running Shoes." Choose the best answer.

Sample

1 The class giggles at Sophy. What can you infer?

  ● They giggle because Sophy is a girl.

  Ⓑ They giggle because Sophy wears running shoes.

  Ⓒ They giggle because Sophy is from Andong Kralong.

  Ⓓ They giggle because Sophy walks barefoot into the classroom.

2 What happens after Sophy's first day of school?

  Ⓐ Sophy wins a race against the boys.

  Ⓑ Sophy's father teaches her to read her name.

  Ⓒ Sophy announces that she wants to learn to read.

  Ⓓ The postal van drops off a package by Sophy's door.

3 What does Sophy's mother think of when she lets Sophy go to school?

  Ⓐ the eight kilometers Sophy will have to run everyday

  Ⓑ Sophy and her father

  Ⓒ Sophy's new shoes

  Ⓓ the number man

 How did you use the test-taking strategy to answer the question?

Name _____ Date _____

"Running Shoes"

Make a story map for "Running Shoes."

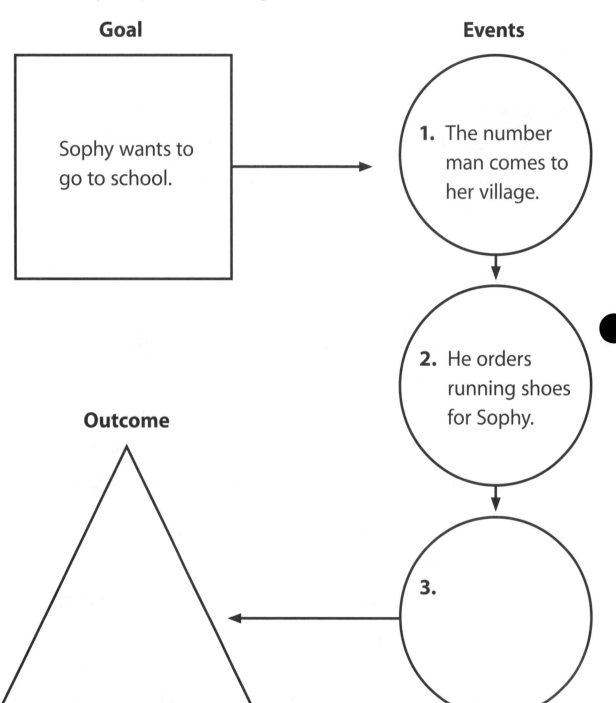

Goal

Sophy wants to go to school.

Events

1. The number man comes to her village.

2. He orders running shoes for Sophy.

3.

Outcome

 Use your story map to talk with a partner about how Sophy achieves her goal.

Fluency Practice

"Running Shoes"

Use this passage to practice reading with proper intonation.

"Running shoes!" she yelled. She carefully put	7
on each shoe. "Now my wish will come true."	16
"What wish?" her mother asked.	21
"I want to go to school."	27
"But the school is eight kilometers away over horrible roads."	37
"Yes, but now I have running shoes!" Sophy	45
said as she bounced up and down.	52

From "Running Shoes," page 496

Intonation

1 ☐ Does not change pitch.   3 ☐ Changes pitch to match some of the content.

2 ☐ Changes pitch, but does not match content.   4 ☐ Changes pitch to match all of the content.

Accuracy and Rate Formula
Use the formula to measure a reader's accuracy and rate while reading aloud.

$$\underline{\hspace{3cm}} - \underline{\hspace{3cm}} = \underline{\hspace{3cm}}$$

| words attempted in one minute | number of errors | words correct per minute (wcpm) |

Grammar: Reteach

Family Outing

Grammar Rules Past-Tense Verbs

A **past-tense** verb tells about an action that happened in the past.	
Just add -**ed** to most verbs to form the past tense.	start + ed = start<u>ed</u>
If a verb ends in silent <u>e</u>, drop the <u>e</u> and add -**ed**.	surpris<del>e</del> + ed = surpris<u>ed</u>
If a one-syllable verb ends in one vowel and one consonant, double the final consonant and add -**ed**.	flip + p + ed = flipp<u>ed</u>
If a verb ends in a consonant and **y**, change the y to i and add -**ed**.	repl<del>y</del> + i + ed = repl<u>ied</u>
If a verb ends in a vowel and **y**, add -**ed**.	delay + ed = delay<u>ed</u>

Read each sentence. Write the correct past-tense verb on the line.

1. My big brother and I _____ three miles to Silver Lake.
       (bike)

2. We _____ there at noon after biking for 40 minutes.
       (arrive)

3. We were so thirsty we _____ our one-liter water bottles.
       (empty)

4. Then we _____ and _____ for an hour.
       (walk)   (climb)

5. We got home at 8 p.m. because a storm _____ us.
       (delay)

 Tell a partner about an outing. Use past-tense verbs with –ed.

Grammar: Game

Connect the Verbs

Directions:

1. Copy the grid below on gray and white paper and cut out the verb cards. Mix up the gray cards and spread them out face down. Mix up the white cards and spread them out face down near the gray cards.

2. Take turns turning over one gray card and one white card. Read aloud the verbs on the cards.

3. Are the words forms of the same verb? If not, turn them face down again.

4. If the words are forms of the same verb, use the past-tense form of the verb in a sentence. For example, if you match *do, does* and *did*, use *did* in a sentence.

5. If you made a match and used the past-tense correctly, keep the cards. If not, put the cards back. The player with more cards at the end of the game wins.

do, does	do, does	did	did
have, has	have, has	had	had
am, is	am, is	was	was
are	are	were	were

Grammar: Game

From Present to Past

Directions:

1. With your group, write each word below on a separate card. Shuffle the cards and stack them face down.

2. Take turns turning over the top card.

3. Spell the past tense of the verb on your card and use it in a sentence. If your group agrees that you are correct, keep the card. If the group is not sure, check the word in a dictionary. If you were wrong, replace the card in the stack.

4. The game ends when all the cards have been taken. The player with the most cards wins.

become	do	are	has
say	know	read	is
achieve	reply	stop	choose
find	have	does	am

Comparison Chart

Compare Settings

Compare the settings in "Three Golden Apples" and "Turtle and His Four Cousins."

	"Three Golden Apples"	**"Turtle and His Four Cousins"**
Where	Greece	
When		

 Talk with a partner about the stories. Tell which story character you liked best and why.

Grammar: Practice

After School

Grammar Rules Verb Tenses: Present and Past

Use present tense to tell about an action that happens now or happens often.

Use past tense to tell about an action that already happened.

Present tense ➡ **I run** three kilometers every day.

Past tense ➡ **I ran** three kilometers yesterday.

Fill in the blanks with present-tense or past-tense verbs.

Every day after school, I _____ soccer. Yesterday, we
⠀⠀⠀⠀⠀⠀⠀⠀⠀⠀⠀⠀⠀⠀⠀(play)

_____ a game. At first, I _____ nothing. I _____ on
⠀⠀(play)⠀⠀⠀⠀⠀⠀⠀⠀⠀⠀⠀⠀⠀(do)⠀⠀⠀⠀⠀⠀⠀⠀⠀(am)

the bench. I _____ my friends. Then the coach _____ over
⠀⠀⠀⠀⠀⠀⠀⠀⠀(watch)⠀⠀⠀⠀⠀⠀⠀⠀⠀⠀⠀⠀⠀⠀⠀⠀(run)

to me.

"Maria," she said, "You always _____ fast. You always
⠀⠀⠀⠀⠀⠀⠀⠀⠀⠀⠀⠀⠀⠀⠀⠀⠀⠀(run)

_____ the ball well. We _____ you now."
⠀(kick)⠀⠀⠀⠀⠀⠀⠀⠀⠀⠀⠀(need)

I _____ out on the field. I _____ a goal! Our team
⠀⠀(go)⠀⠀⠀⠀⠀⠀⠀⠀⠀⠀⠀⠀⠀(score)

_____ the winner!
⠀(is)

 Tell a partner about something you did yesterday and something you do almost every day. Use past-tense and present-tense verbs.

Name _____ Date _____

Rambé and Ambé
Trick the Cat
a Tibetan folk tale retold by Alice McDonnell

Characters
CAT **AMBÉ**, a mouse
RAMBÉ, a mouse Other **MICE**

SCENE ONE

[**SETTING** *A fat old* CAT *lives in an old farmhouse in Tibet's icy Himalaya Mountains long ago.*]

CAT [*to herself*]: So many mice, and yet I'm hungry! I used to catch all the mice I wanted, but now I'm old and slow. They are too quick for me. It's freezing outside, so I can't hunt in the snow. I need a strategy to put the mice off guard. [CAT *thinks, then smiles nastily.*]

SCENE TWO

[*Next morning, nervous* MICE *surround* CAT.]

CAT [*sincerely*]: Neighbor Mice, I am sorry for my past wickedness. I have decided to change my ways. From now on, you can run about with no fear. I will not even *try* to catch you. All I ask is this: twice a day, you must all walk past me in a line and bow to show your gratitude.

[*The* MICE *cheer and talk excitedly to one another.*]

MICE: Neighbor Cat, we accept your kind offer.

[*MICE parade by, bowing to* CAT *who waits calmly. As the last mouse bows to her, she pounces and gobbles it down without the others noticing.*]

> **Viewpoints:** _____
> _____
> _____

Mark-Up Reading

Rambé and Ambé
Trick the Cat (continued)

SCENE THREE

[*Several days later,* CAT's *strategy has worked.* RAMBÉ *and* AMBÉ *talk nervously.*]

RAMBÉ: Have you noticed that mice have been disappearing?

AMBÉ [*angry*]: I *knew* we shouldn't trust Cat. She must be up to something!

RAMBÉ [*now also angry*]: I think I have a plan.

[RAMBÉ *and* AMBÉ *put their heads together and whisper quietly.*]

SCENE FOUR

[*Next morning, the* MICE *walk by* CAT, *bowing respectfully as they pass.* RAMBÉ *leads and* AMBÉ *is the last mouse in line.*]

RAMBÉ [*bows to* CAT, *then looks toward the end of the line*]: Where are you, friend Ambé?

AMBÉ [*waving excitedly*]: Here I am, here I am, friend Rambé!

[*The two mice call cheerfully to one another, back and forth. All the* MICE *watch* AMBÉ *until he passes* CAT *safely.*]

CAT [*mutters angrily*]: What a racket! How can I be expected to eat the last mouse with everyone looking? But this must be an accident! This afternoon those two will be in the middle of the line, and I will find a nice, fat mouse at the end!

Explain Viewpoints: _____

_____

_____

_____

Mark-Up Reading

Rambé and Ambé
Trick the Cat (continued)

SCENE FIVE

[*That afternoon,* CAT *is furious to find that* RAMBÉ *and* AMBÉ *are again in the same positions. Once more, the two friends exchange noisy, cheerful greetings and* AMBÉ *escapes.*]

RAMBÉ [*grimly to* AMBÉ *when they meet later*]: I wonder how long Cat will put up with this game. Sooner or later she's sure to "smell a rat," if you'll pardon the expression. But we've got to beat her!

SCENE SIX

[*Next morning,* CAT *is hungry and desperate. When* RAMBÉ *and* AMBÉ *start their game again,* CAT *leaps furiously at all the* MICE, *but they easily scamper out of reach of her claws.* CAT *hisses and spits in anger.*]

RAMBÉ [*boldly, from a safe distance*]: Cat, how many times do you think you could fool us? We now know better than to ever trust you again!

CAT [*now tearful from hunger and frustration*]: You are all wicked to treat a poor old neighbor in this way! I'll never speak to any of you again!

AMBÉ [*laughing at* RAMBÉ's *side*]: That works for us! Enjoy the great outdoors.

Explain Viewpoints: _____

_____

_____

_____

_____

_____

Grammar: Grammar and Writing

Edit and Proofread

Choose the Editing and Proofreading Marks you need to correct the passage. Look for correct usage of the following:

- regular past-tense verbs
- irregular past-tense verbs

Editing and Proofreading Marks

∧	Add.
♪	Take out.
≡	Capitalize.
⊙	Add period.
⋏	Add comma.

Last week, Atalanta ~~readed~~ *read* about a turtle who raced a deer—and won! She wantted to race Turtle, so she and Melanion went to Cuba.

They finded Turtle crawling on the beach. How did this turtle beat a deer? "What is the secret of your speed?" Melanion askd. Turtle just shruged, but he agreed to a race.

After Atalanta and Melanion left, Turtle called his cousins. They divideed the route again.

The next day, Atalanta were on the beach. Melanion had gone to the finish line to wait. Guess who he surpriseed? "I knowed you had a secret!" sayed Melanion. Turtle replyed, "I have cousins along the route." When Atalanta arrived, all three enjoied a laugh. "It was a clever trick!" admitted Atalanta.

Name _____ Date _____

Grab Your Kite!

Grammar Rules Past-Tense Verbs

A **past-tense** verb tells about an action that happened in the past.

Use rules to form **regular past-tense verbs.**

follow + <u>ed</u> = follow<u>ed</u>   repl<u>y</u> + <u>i</u> + <u>ed</u> = repl<u>ied</u>

wad<u>e</u> + <u>ed</u> = wad<u>ed</u>   t<u>ip</u> + <u>p</u> + <u>ed</u> = tip<u>ped</u>

ob<u>ey</u> + <u>ed</u> = obey<u>ed</u>

Learn **irregular past-tense verbs.**

am, is, are ➔ was, were   become ➔ became   eat ➔ ate

come ➔ came   do, does ➔ did   say ➔ said

go, goes ➔ went   have, has ➔ had   read ➔ read

choose ➔ chose   find ➔ found   know ➔ knew

Read paragraph A. In paragraph B, write the past-tense form of each underlined verb.

A. Today <u>is</u> very windy. We <u>try</u> to fly our kites. My friend's kite <u>drops</u> hard, and it <u>comes</u> close to the ground. My kite <u>surprises</u> me. It <u>does</u> a funny swoop, and then it <u>flips</u>!

B. Yesterday _____ very windy. We _____ to fly our kites. My friend's kite _____ hard, and it _____ close to the ground. My kite _____ me. It _____ a funny swoop, and then it _____!

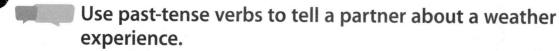 **Use past-tense verbs to tell a partner about a weather experience.**

Interesting Places

Make a main idea diagram about the main idea: There are many interesting places to visit.

Main Idea

There are many interesting places to visit.

Details

Take turns with your partner telling more details that could support the main idea.

Grammar: Game

Irregular Travel

Directions:

1. **Imagine your travel plans:** Would you like to travel on a flying carpet or grab a ride on a whale? Think of unusual ways to travel. Play with a partner. First, tell your partner how you're traveling.

2. **Take turns spinning:** Spin for a verb. Read aloud the verb and then say and spell its past-tense form.

3. **Use the past-tense verb:** Remember to tell how you're traveling. Then use the past-tense verb to tell something about your trip. Example: *I traveled to Alaska on a dolphin and the cold water froze my cellphone.*

4. **Score:** If you spelled and used the past-tense verb correctly, score one point. The player with the most points after six rounds wins the game.

Verbs

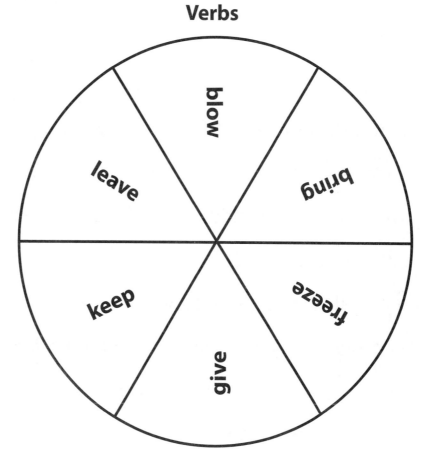

Make a Spinner

1. Put a paper clip over the center of the spinner.
2. Put a pencil point through a loop of the paper clip.
3. Hold the pencil firmly with one hand. Spin the paper clip with the other hand.

Grammar: Grammar and Writing

Edit and Proofread

Choose the Editing and Proofreading Marks you need to correct the passage. Look for correct usage of the following:

- irregular past-tense verbs
- subject-verb agreement

Editing and Proofreading Marks

∧	Add.
৶	Take out.
≡	Capitalize.
⊙	Add period.
⅄	Add comma.

                                                  was

I remember my first camping trip like it ~~are~~ yesterday. My dad, brother, and I leaved our home in the city on a Saturday morning. On the way, we stopped at a grocery store and buyed food. My dad bringed all of our camping supplies in the back of his truck. As we rided up the winding mountain road, we seen many amazing views.

When we got to the campground, my brother and I helped our dad pitch the tent. After our campsite are ready, we went on a hike. But when we is in the middle of the forest, my dad stopped. He looked in his bag. "I thought I have a compass in here," he said. "Uh oh," my brother said. "I taked it yesterday to my friend's house."

"Don't worry," my dad said. "I can get us back to our campsite in no time." He does his best, but it still took us over an hour!

Test-Taking Strategy Practice

Skip and Return to Questions

Read each question about "One Man's Goal."
Choose the best answer.

Sample

1. What message is Eruç trying to teach students?
   - ● Never give up on your dreams.
   - Ⓑ Traveling can be dangerous.
   - Ⓒ Always take a music player with you.

2. What motivated Eruç to climb on six continents?
   - Ⓐ his love of high places
   - Ⓑ the daily challenges he faces
   - Ⓒ the memory of a hiker friend

3. Why did Eruç go to Papua New Guinea?
   - Ⓐ There was a mountain to climb there.
   - Ⓑ The wind and rain pushed him there.
   - Ⓒ He needed to fix his boat there.

4. What is one way Eruç did not travel?
   - Ⓐ by boat
   - Ⓑ by car
   - Ⓒ by bike

How did you use the test test-taking strategy to answer the question?

Name _____ Date _____

"One Man's Goal"

Make a main idea diagram for different sections of "One Man's Goal."

Main Idea	**Details**
	He left California in a boat in 2007.
Eruç decided to go around the world.	He rowed across the Pacific Ocean to Australia.

 Use your main idea diagrams to summarize parts of the selection for a partner.

Fluency Practice

"One Man's Goal"

Use this passage to practice reading with proper phrasing.

Crossing the Pacific was amazing, but that was only part of Eruç's	12
journey. He was determined to go around the world—using his	23
own energy!	25
During his journey, Eruç wanted to climb the tallest peaks on six	37
continents to honor the memory of a fellow climber. Eruç planned to bike,	50
walk, climb, and row the world—without any motors to help him.	62

From "One Man's Goal," page 529

Phrasing

1 ☐ Rarely pauses while reading the text.   3 ☐ Frequently pauses at appropriate points in the text.

2 ☐ Occasionally pauses while reading the text.   4 ☐ Consistently pauses at all appropriate points in the text.

Accuracy and Rate Formula
Use the formula to measure a reader's accuracy and rate while reading aloud.

$$\underbrace{\rule{3cm}{0.4pt}}_{\substack{\text{words attempted} \\ \text{in one minute}}} - \underbrace{\rule{3cm}{0.4pt}}_{\text{number of errors}} = \underbrace{\rule{3cm}{0.4pt}}_{\substack{\text{words correct per minute} \\ \text{(wcpm)}}}$$

Name _____ Date _____

It Was a New View!

Grammar Rules Irregular Past-Tense Forms

A **past-tense** verb tells about an action that happened in the past.

Irregular past-tense verbs have special forms to learn.

am, is, are ➛ **was, were**	do, does ➛ **did**	have, has ➛ **had**
begin ➛ **began**	blow ➛ **blew**	bring ➛ **brought**
buy ➛ **bought**	come ➛ **came**	freeze ➛ **froze**
give ➛ **gave**	keep ➛ **kept**	leave ➛ **left**
ride ➛ **rode**	see ➛ **saw**	take ➛ **took**

Write the correct verb forms on the blank lines.

1. Last week, we _____ in a hot-air balloon!
     (are)

2. We _____ in a park and floated toward the clouds.
     (begin)

3. We _____ patchwork fields with crops and cows!
     (see)

4. A wind _____ us over town, and we _____ photos.
     (blows)   (take)

5. Our trip _____ us a bird's eye view of our town.
     (gives)

6. We _____ in the balloon all afternoon.
     (ride)

7. The pilot _____ us down, and we _____ the balloon.
     (bring)   (leave)

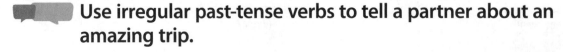 Use irregular past-tense verbs to tell a partner about an amazing trip.

Grammar: Game

Into the Future!

To Prepare:

1. Work in a group. Write each subject with its verb on a card.

2. Mix up the cards, and place them face down in a stack.

To Play:

1. Take turns turning over the top card. Read the subject and verb.

2. Then use the subject and future tense in a sentence. For example, if you choose the card *I discover*, say: *I will discover a new island.*

3. If the group agrees that you have used the future tense correctly, keep the card. If not, put the card at the bottom of the stack. The player with the most cards at the end of the game wins.

He rides	**We climbed**	**I discover**	**We estimate**
They started	**He found**	**You took**	**She achieves**
She rows	**I explored**	**He began**	**It froze**
It travels	**You fly**	**They pack**	**She chose**

Grammar: Game

Who Will Reach the Top First?

Directions:

1. Write *will*, *am going to*, *is going to*, and *are going to* on index cards. Mix them up, and stack them face down.

2. Take turns flipping a coin. For heads, move two squares; for tails, move one.

3. Pick a card. Read the card and the verb in the square. Then use them in a sentence. Place the card at the bottom of the stack.

4. If your sentence is correct, stay where you are. If not, go back one.

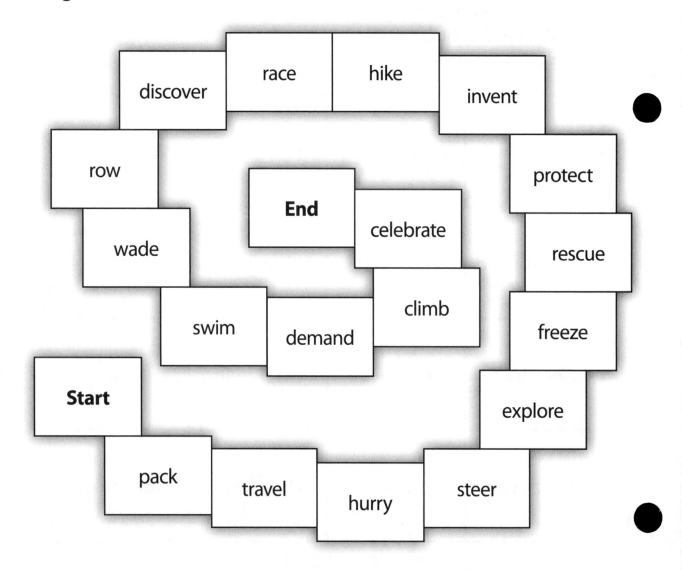

Name _____ Date _____

Compare Causes

Compare Erden Eruç and Constanza Ceruti.

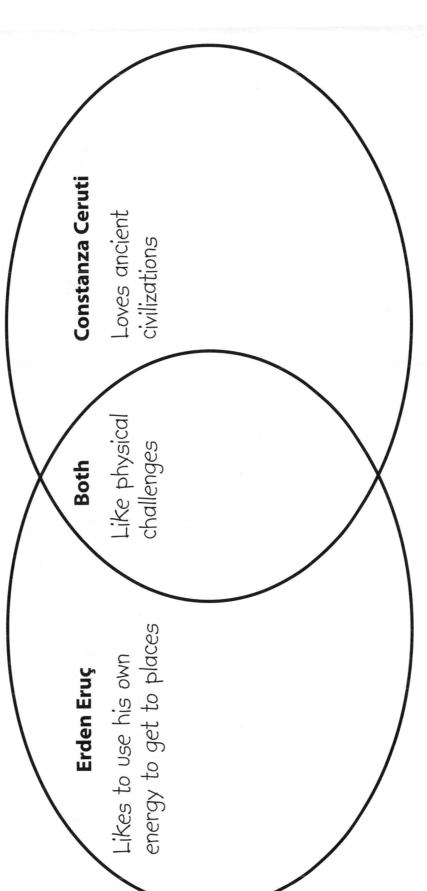

Erden Eruç

Likes to use his own energy to get to places

Both

Like physical challenges

Constanza Ceruti

Loves ancient civilizations

Take turns with a partner. Tell about one thing that caused each person to begin an adventure.

For use with TE p. T545a   **PM8.27**   **Unit 8** | Getting There

Name _____ Date _____

Grammar: Practice

A Busy Weekend

Grammar Rules Future Tense

You can show the future tense in two different ways:	
Use *will* + a main verb	I **will make** tacos tonight.
Use *am/is/are* + *going to* + a main verb	I **am going to make** tacos tonight.

Each sentence tells about a future action. Rewrite the verb in each sentence to show a different way to say the same thing.

1. I will study for my math test this weekend.

   I _____ for my math test this weekend.

2. My sister is going to practice her basketball skills.

   My sister _____ her basketball skills.

3. My brothers will prepare their science project.

   My brothers _____ their science project.

4. My mother is going to help Aunt Sally move to a new home.

   My mother _____ Aunt Sally move to a new home.

5. It will be a very busy weekend.

   It _____ a very busy weekend.

 Tell your partner what your friends or family members will probably do this weekend. Use *will* or *going to*.

Name _____ Date _____

Searching for *Titanic*
BY MARIA BERTSCH

The first time Dr. Robert Ballard explored the ocean, he got quite a thrill. He was on an ocean research voyage when a huge wave nearly sank his ship. Others might have been frightened off by this incident. The result for Ballard was that he was "hooked for life."

▲ Dr. Robert Ballard, the man who found the *Titanic* shipwreck

CAUSE		EFFECT
A huge wave nearly sank Ballard's ship.	→	_____ _____

Ballard became an ocean explorer and undersea craft designer. In 1985, he developed *Argo*, an unmanned submarine. Since he needed to test it, he decided to use *Argo* to look for the world's most famous shipwreck—*Titanic*. Ballard was determined to find this great ship.

CAUSE		EFFECT
_____ _____	→	Ballard decided to test *Argo* by looking for *Titanic*.

Because *Titanic* sank in such deep water, people believed it could not be reached. Special equipment was needed that could hold up under the high water pressure. Ballard's *Argo* was built for high pressures.

CAUSE	EFFECT
Titanic sank in very deep water.	_____ _____
	EFFECT
	_____ _____

Mark-Up Reading

Searching for *Titanic* (continued)
BY MARIA BERTSCH

Argo was well-suited to its job. It had video cameras that Ballard's crew could control remotely. Still, Ballard had only twelve days for his search. He believed that when *Titanic* sank it left a trail of wreckage on the ocean floor. So he would use *Argo* to look for these pieces and follow them to *Titanic*.

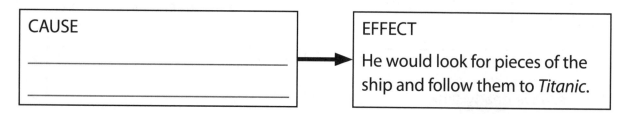

CAUSE		EFFECT
_____ _____	→	He would look for pieces of the ship and follow them to *Titanic*.

Ballard and his team worked day and night, searching for any sign of the ship. *Argo's* cameras took videos of the ocean floor. At first, they just saw a lot of mud. Then metal objects began to show up. Finally, a crew member spotted one of the sunken ship's huge boilers. As a result, Ballard's team knew they had found *Titanic*.

CAUSE		EFFECT
A crew member spotted one of the ship's huge boilers.	→	_____ _____

After his discovery, Ballard received thousands of letters from students inspired by his work. As a result, Ballard created the JASON Project. It is an education program that connects students with scientists. Still, Ballard could never desert his first love–exploration. As long as there is an ocean, he will continue to unlock its secrets.

CAUSE		EFFECT
_____ _____	→	Ballard started the JASON Project to connect students with scientists.

Grammar: Grammar and Writing

Edit and Proofread

Choose the Editing and Proofreading Marks you need to correct the passage. Look for correct usage of the following:

- future-tense verbs

Editing and Proofreading Marks

∧	Add.
✐	Take out.
≡	Capitalize.
⊙	Add period.
⋀	Add comma.

Constanza Ceruti will climbed many miles in freezing weather

to find ancient things. She once found 500-year-old mummies!

Next weekend, my family is going drive to another city to see

ancient things. We will finds things that are 500 years old, too.

None of us will froze, though! We is going to visit a museum!

The museum has objects that are hundreds of years old. My

parents like handmade things, so they going to see colonial

furniture. My sister is going to look at clothes. She will studies

fashion design next year. I is going to explore navigation tools.

Someday I will piloted a big ship, like an ocean liner. I wonder what

everyday things from my life will be in museums in the future!

Grammar: Reteach

A Nature Hike in Our Future

Grammar Rules Future Tense

A **future tense verb** tells about an action that will happen later, or in the future.

Future tense is shown with:	We <u>will</u> `hike` on a nature trail.
• the helping verb <u>will</u> and a `main verb`	I <u>am going to</u> `plan` a picnic lunch.
	He <u>is going to</u> `ask` for a map.
• the phrase <u>am going to</u>, <u>is going to</u>, or <u>are going to</u> before a `main verb`	You <u>are going to</u> `meet` us.
	They <u>are going to</u> `join` us, too.

Read each sentence. Read the clue after the sentence. Then use the clue to write the future tense of the underlined verb.

1. We <u>choose</u> a trail around a pond. (will) _____

2. I <u>see</u> tadpoles and tree toads. (going to) _____

3. Emma <u>brings</u> a book on flowers. (will) _____

4. Our nature guide <u>names</u> trees and birds. (will) _____

5. We <u>discover</u> song birds on the trail. (going to) _____

6. José <u>carries</u> a magnifying glass. (going to) _____

7. He <u>studies</u> insects of all sizes. (going to) _____

8. You <u>tell</u> everyone to walk quietly. (will) _____

9. Otherwise, the animals <u>hide</u> from us. (will) _____

▬▬▬ **Use future-tense verbs to tell a partner about an outdoor activity you would like to do.**